EXHORTATIONS OF JESUS ACCORDING TO MATTHEW
and
UP FROM THE DEPTHS

Mark As Tragedy

Morris A. Inch

University Press of America, Inc.
Lanham • New York • Oxford

Copyright © 1997 by
University Press of America,® Inc.
4720 Boston Way
Lanham, Maryland 20706

12 Hid's Copse Rd.
Cummor Hill, Oxford OX2 9JJ

All rights reserved
Printed in the United States of America
British Library Cataloguing in Publication Information Available

Library of Congress Cataloging-in-Publication

Inch, Morris A.
Exhortations of Jesus according to Matthew ; and, Up from the depths :
Mark as tragedy / Morris A. Inch.
p. cm.
Includes bibliographical references and indexes.
1. Jesus Christ--Words. 2. Bible. N.T. Matthew--Criticism,
interpretation, etc. 3. Jesus Christ--Messiahship. 4. Bible. N.T.
Mark--Criticism, interpretation, etc. I. Title. II. Title: Up from the
depths.
BT306.I53   1997   226.2'06--dc21   97-1466 CIP

ISBN 0-7618-0696-2 (cloth: alk. ppr.)
ISBN 0-7618-0697-0 (pbk: alk. ppr.)

∞™ The paper used in this publication meets the minimum
requirements of American National Standard for information
Sciences—Permanence of Paper for Printed Library Materials,
ANSI Z39.48—1984

CONTENTS

Acknowledgment		v
Exhortations of Jesus According to Matthew--Part I		vii
Preface		ix
Chapter 1	Overview	1
Chapter 2	The Messiah	9
Chapter 3	The Kingdom of Heaven (God)	17
Chapter 4	The Scriptures	25
Chapter 5	The Community	33
Chapter 6	Its Mission	43
Chapter 7	The Consummation	51
Epilogue		59
Endnotes		63
Bibliography		65
Index		67

Up From the Depths--Part II

Preface		71
Chapter 1	Tragic Hero	73
Chapter 2	Tragic Flaw	81
Chapter 3	Tragic Design	89
Chapter 4	Tragic Consequence	97
Chapter 5	Reality	105
Chapter 6	Suffering	113
Chapter 7	Courage	121
Chapter 8	Oracles	129
Chapter 9	Facing Up To Fear	137
Chapter 10	Experiencing Pity	145
Chapter 11	Catharsis	153
Chapter 12	Bottom Line	163
Endnotes		169
Bibliography		171
Index		175

Acknowledgment

A special word of appreciation to my ever supportive wife Joan, and our devoted son Thomas, who formatted and prepared the text for publication. This being a family project has made it more satisfying.

Part I

EXHORTATIONS OF JESUS ACCORDING TO MATTHEW

PREFACE

In the discussion to follow, we will consider the Messianic *paraklesis* (exhortation) as recorded in Matthew's gospel. As far as I am aware, this topic has previously been considered only incidentally and with little elaboration.

The admonitions of Jesus may be thought of as a prelude to Christian ethics. As such, more time spent this way would yield better results long term.

On the other hand, the Messianic *paraklesis* constitutes an incipient ethic in itself. It already provides the focus and sets the perimeters of investigation.

Matthew was a logical choice. Ernest Renan, the popular nineteenth century biographer of Jesus, concluded that Matthew was the most important book ever written. Whether one agrees with his estimate or not, Matthew has uniformly introduced the New Testament corpus, and was especially prized by the early church.

In addition and more to the point, Matthew gives the most thorough attention to Jesus' exhortations. It records about 70% of the data either alone or with one or both of the other Synoptic Gospels (Mark and Luke).

Earlier on, I published concerning Matthew's Gospel, *Celebrating Jesus as Lord*. I attempted on that occasion to demonstrate that the reasons reported for Matthew being popular in the early house church movement ought to make it particularly relevant for today. No challenge to this thesis has come to my attention.

This, then, is for me like coming home to familiar surroundings. If I should betray some enthusiasm from time to time, it is probably genuine. Good reading!

Chapter 1

OVERVIEW

After relocating in Capernaum from Nazareth, Jesus began to preach: "Repent, for the kingdom of heaven is near" (4:17). While this echoes the message of John the Baptist, Jesus identified the approach of the kingdom with His life and ministry. The implications of this will become evident as the discussion progresses.

Jesus solicited a decisive response, as illustrated by His call of Simon (Peter), and Simon's brother Andrew. As Jesus walked by the Sea of Galilee, He observed them casting their net. "Come, follow me," Jesus encouraged them, "and I will make you fishers of men" (4:19). "At once they left their nets and followed him."

Going on from there, Jesus saw two other brothers: James and John, sons of Zebedee. They were fixing their nets. When Jesus called them, they immediately left the boat and their father and followed Him.

This was obviously a momentous occasion that would take priority over the natural pursuits of life. All else would have to be recast in the light of God's most recent initiative. Despite the outcome, these fledgling disciples would follow after (come behind) Jesus.

From A Mountainside

Jesus proceeded throughout Galilee, teaching in its synagogues, preaching the good news of the kingdom, and healing all manner of sickness. His ministry involved exposition, proclamation, and healing. The expression "good news" was used as a succinct summary of Jesus' teaching (cf. 9:35; 24:14).

Large crowds from Galilee, the Decapolis, Judea (including

Jerusalem), and the Transjordan flocked after the rabbi from Nazareth by way of Capernaum. Now when Jesus saw the multitude, he went up on a mountainside and (as was the custom) sat to teach. His disciples came to Him, attentive to what He had to say.

The crowd watched and strained to hear, catching what crumbs they could from the disciples' table. As Dietrich Bonhoeffer was want to say: "Jesus taught His disciples in the presence of the multitude."

The initial cast was assembled: Jesus, His disciples, and the multitude. "Jesus" ("Yahweh saves") was an exceedingly common name for a thoroughly uncommon person. Five high priests bore that name. In the works of Josephus, about twenty persons were called Jesus, perhaps ten of them contemporary to the Master.

Matthew does not think any physical characteristic of Jesus worth noting. We can surmise that He was sturdy of build, given His vocation and the taxing demands of His ministry. He could project His voice to take advantage of a natural amphitheater, and be heard by a great audience. Otherwise, there was little that would distinguish Jesus' appearance or decorum from other Jews of the time. (There were definite standards regarding outward appearance of a proper Jew, and especially any that lay claim to being a rabbi.)

Jesus was Galilean. He spoke in a course dialect, thought displeasing by those who dwelt in and around Jerusalem. Galileans also were characterized by a fierce, independent spirit that cherished ideals over comfort. Nothing in Matthew's account would lead us to think that Jesus was an exception to the rule.

He was acclaimed a rabbi (teacher). Even so, His education seems not to have extended beyond that available in Nazareth. He would have been therefore considered "unschooled", as were His disciples (cf. Acts 4:13). People were amazed with His teaching, primarily because He taught authoritatively instead of by precedent--as was rabbinic practice.

He was no doubt charismatic, in the sense of being endowed, and inciting loyalty and devotion among His followers. They were prepared to follow Him come the proverbial "hell or high water."

Jesus began His public ministry at about thirty years of age. He had bided His time until culturally acceptable to carry on His itinerant ministry. He seems always sensitive to cultural matters, as He was to individuals.

As we have seen, Jesus began to call out disciples: Peter, Andrew, James, and John. There were countless others; twelve including the above formed an inner circle.

Discipleship at first involved going where Jesus went, sharing in His joys and privations. When Jesus went among the outcasts to minister, the disciples accompanied Him. When He went into a deserted place to pray, the disciples followed after Him. He was their role model; they patterned their lives after Him.

It was for Jesus to command; His disciples to obey. They were not passive but compliant. The former implies a lack of personal involvement, while the disciples put their all into it.

They forsook all, the good and the bad alike. The disciples would from that moment forward live in fellowship with Christ. They would gladly surrender their autonomy.

They embraced all, for better and for worse. Whatever the benefits of discipleship, they would reap them. Whatever the cost of discipleship, they would assume it.

The call to discipleship proved to be a call to community. The disciple found himself among others of like commitment. The fellowship would eventually come to differ in seemingly every other regard: racially, socially, economically, and dispositionally. It would become, as portrayed by the prominent church historian Kenneth Scott Latourette, a cross-section of society.

Finally, there was the multitude. It constituted the vast majority. Jesus enjoined those within the sound of His voice: "Enter through the narrow gate. For wide is the gate and broad is the road that leads to destruction, and many enter through it. But small is the gate and narrow the road that leads to life, and only a few find it" (7:13-14).

The multitude was mixed. Some were simply curious, others desperate, still others seeking. Some shifted as time wore on, either for the better or the worse.

The multitude was inclined to vacillate, depending on circumstances or how others were disposed. At times, it swept Jesus along with its acclaim. On other occasions, it turned adversarial. One could never be certain which way the wind would blow or how long it would prevail.

The disciples were drawn from the multitude. They could understand what it was like to walk in darkness. They were summoned to become the light of the world.

Rabbi, disciples, and multitude--these three gathered on a mountainside overlooking the sparkling Sea of Galilee. Jesus' reputation had drawn them there. His words would hold their attention. One holds his/her breath in anticipation for the events to follow.

Messianic Exhortations

The *paraklesis* can be subsumed under six categories: concerning the Messiah, kingdom of heaven (God), the scriptures, community, its mission, and the consummation. To admit some overlap would be to state the obvious.

The Messiah. "Come follow me," Jesus bid the fishermen. The call bridged between Jesus' Messianic temptation and ministry. The Messianic context provides the clue for our understanding.

John had promised: "After me will come one who is more powerful than I, whose sandals I am not fit to carry. ...His winnowing fork is in his hand, and he will clear his threshing floor, gathering his wheat into the barn and burning up the chaff with unquenchable fire" (3:11-12). Give heed to what He has to say.

As the one anticipated, Jesus exhorted those around Him. He urged them to forsake their sin and pursue righteousness. He encouraged them to take advantage of God's Messianic initiative. As Paul would put it: "Now is the time of God's favor, now is the day of salvation" (2 Cor. 6:2).

Kingdom of heaven. As noted earlier, Jesus came preaching: "Repent, for the kingdom of heaven is at hand" (4:17). Repent, because time is running out. Repent, because of the opportunity afforded. Repent, because of what stands to be lost. Repent, if for no other reason than God would have you do so.

On another occasion, Jesus exhorted His audience: "Seek first his kingdom and his righteousness, and all these things will be given to you as well" (6:33). Do not be anxious concerning the affairs of life. God is well aware of your needs and concerned to meet them. Put first things first, and trust Him to meet your needs. In this and other ways, Jesus admonished folk concerning the kingdom.

The scriptures. When tempted by the devil, Jesus replied: "It is written" (4:4,5,10). He did not say this to exhort others, except by example. He bore witness to living each day in accordance with the teachings of Holy Writ.

He was not reluctant to encourage others in this regard, or to criticize them when they strayed. On one occasion, He complained: "Thus you nullify the word of God for the sake of your tradition" (15:6). Inspired teaching must always take precedence over human predilection.

Community. Why of all the things Jesus did and said have the gospel writers preserved what they have passed down to us? A major factor appears to have been its continuing relevance for the Christian community. These were matters of abiding communal concern.

As a case in point, Jesus advocated: "If you are offering your gift at the altar and there remember that your brother has something against you, leave your gift there in front of the altar. First go and be reconciled to your brother; then come and offer your gift" (5:23-24). Worship ought not to be used as an escape from community but as an expression of it.

Its mission. The disciples were to come together in worship and go in service. This coming and going was to characterize their life together. While certain of Jesus' exhortations pertained to the former, others related to the latter.

Jesus had set the pattern from the beginning. Calling persons to Himself, He sent them forth to disciple others. As for those who were fishermen by vocation, He announced that they would become fishers of men (cf. 4:19).

On another occasion, Jesus observed that the harvest was plentiful but the workers few. Then He admonished the disciples: "Ask the Lord of the harvest, therefore, to send out workers into his harvest field" (9:38). Go and pray that the Lord send others to join in the labor.

The consummation. Jesus encouraged persons not to take a truncated view of life. Live with eternity in view.

Since we may tolerate what hinders our spiritual growth, Jesus counseled: "If your hand or your foot causes you to sin, cut it off and throw it away. It is better for you to enter life maimed or crippled than to have two hands or two feet and be thrown into eternal fire" (18:8).

The end is nearer than we may think. It will come unexpectedly, as would a thief in the night. Be prepared!

In these and other ways, Jesus exhorted those who would listen. Some heard words void of meaning. Others drank in what Jesus had to say, as if living (running) water. They were refreshed, and went on their way rejoicing.

Ethical Interpretations

Richard Hires explores four interpretations of Jesus' ethic: ethics without eschatology, ethics and eschatology, ethics as eschatology, and the ethics of realized eschatology.[1] These serve to illustrate diverse ways in which ethical theorists have understood the teaching of Jesus.

Carl Gustav Adolf Von Harnack is representative of the *ethics without eschatology* option. He hoped to revive an interest in ethics at some expense to dogma. In particular, he wanted to preserve the ethical kernel of Jesus' teaching apart from its eschatological husk.

Harnack variously described what he considered the essence of Jesus' praxis. Most often, he returned to the idea of a person released to love God and others. He meant to accent the kingdom of heaven as presently available to those who would appropriate it.

Harnack was a classic spokesman for Protestant liberalism. While liberalism has come under scathing criticism, it has survived among churchmen of less traditional thinking and more humanistic leaning. It is still a force to be considered.

Albert Sweitzer represents the *ethics and eschatology* alternative. Jesus was, according to Sweitzer, a person of His times, sharing the expectation that the age was drawing to a climactic conclusion. The Son of Man would appear, the dead be raised, the judgment occur, the righteous receive their eternal reward, and the wicked suffer their dismal exclusion. Thus he hoped to revive eschatology.

As for Sweitzer, he discovered the clue to Jesus' ethic in the sanctity of life. He concluded that Jesus spoke out of a time unfathomable to us but with continuing relevance.

Reverence of life meant for Sweitzer to grasp and devote oneself to the infinite, inexplicable, and forward-urging will of God. To describe his view as "ethical mysticism" seems not far off target. It constituted but one protest against traditional liberalism.

The prominent New Testament scholar Rudolf Bultmann took a different attack on liberalism, with *ethics as eschatology*. Bultmann felt the gospel records too fragmentary and legendary to be of substantial worth in reconstructing historical events. Instead, he emphasized the faith of the early Christians as it has relevance for today.

Bultmann's concern grew out of ministering to those handicapped by their war experience. He searched for a way they might accept the challenge to live courageously in the face of disabling obstacles.

Bultmann scoffed at the idea that modern man could embrace the beliefs of antiquity. As often noted, he claimed that anyone who turns on an electric light could not be expected to believe in miracles. He maintained that we should demythologize the Biblical text, expressing faith in existential terms.

Jesus' ethic, according to Bultmann, consisted of radical obedience to the will of God. Jesus taught no ethics in the sense of a system valid for all time, but left the decision to us in our concrete situation. If a person genuinely loves, Bultmann was confident that he/she already knew what must be done.

C.H. Dodd introduces the final option: *ethics as realized eschatology*. According to Dodd, the kingdom of heaven was actualized with the advent of Jesus as the Christ. It had not simply drawn near but *arrived*. (Not uncommonly overlooked, the English academic came to believe that there remains a residual fulfillment.)

Dodd does not allow for an interim ethic. He reasons that Jesus as a rule spoke to concrete situations. Yet, in that His pronouncements were intended as "dramatic illustrations" of a consistent understanding of God, man, and the world, they may be said to reveal the "absolute standards" by which we shall be judged.[2]

Dodd suggests that Jesus' ideals are not strictly speaking attainable. They perhaps resemble a goal toward which we constantly press. They nonetheless reflect a quality though deficient, and a direction though still distant.

These representative theories arm us with comprehensive alternative approaches to Christian ethics. I have stopped short of suggesting an additional option, being content with such insights as may arise from the historical context.

Even so, I can most readily identify with Dodd of the theories sketched. I especially appreciate his accent on the *sitz en laben* (setting) of Jesus' teaching as pivotal to our ethical understanding. This will become increasingly evident as the discussion develops.

Chapter 2

THE MESSIAH

Matthew meant to establish Jesus' Messianic credentials by inclusion of His genealogical record. It introduces "Jesus Christ" (1:1), and concludes with Mary "of whom was born Jesus, who is called Christ" (1:16).

Jesus allowed that He was the Messiah (Christ, anointed) on various occasions: in response to Peter at Caesarea Philippi (16:16), crowds at His triumphant entry into Jerusalem (21:9), and children in the temple area (21:15). He was reluctant to volunteer the term because it was primarily associated with a political liberator. He chose instead to employ "the Son of Man", a designation less precise and more pliable.

The Messianic Ambiguity

Roman rule fanned the embers of Messianic anticipation. Given time and ingenuity, the rabbis would identify no less than 456 Biblical references to the Deliverer. One could easily imagine devout Jews pouring over the sacred text to add to a growing Messianic legacy.

The Messianic profile nonetheless remained obscure due to seemingly contradictory ingredients, accentuated by personal or corporate preference. On the one hand, it appeared as if God Himself would intervene; on the other, as if through a chosen agent. On the one hand, the Messiah appeared as a military figure; on the other, as a heavenly agent. On the one hand, he was represented as the royal heir to David's throne; on the other, as a suffering servant.

God as Messianic agent or through a chosen alternative? "Behold, I will create new heavens and new earth. The former things will not be remembered, nor will they come to mind" (Isa. 65:17). In another context, "I will give them an undivided heart and put a new spirit in them; I will remove from them their heart of stone and give them a heart of flesh" (Ezek. 11:19). In such instances, we find no hint of an intermediary.

Conversely, "a shoot will come up from the stump of Jesse, from his roots a Branch will bear fruit. ...He will strike the earth with the rod of his mouth; with the breath of his lips he will slay the wicked. Righteousness will be his belt and faithfulness the sash around his waist" (Isa. 11:1,4-5). God will accomplish His purpose through His anointed.

Military deliverer or heavenly agent? "When they cry to the Lord because of their oppressors, he will send them a savior and defender, and he will rescue them" (Isa. 20:1). Much as God raised judges to deliver His people, then for only an interim but henceforth for evermore.

As mentioned earlier, political imagery came to predominate. The astute Jewish writer Samuel Sandmel elaborates:

> The Jewish Messiah was expected to accomplish specific aims. He would destroy the sovereignty of Rome; he would set up a legitimate Jewish kingdom, not of the hated Hasmonean or Herodian stock, but of the genuine Jewish royalty, the stock of King David; he would gather in the exiles from all over the Diaspora; his coming would usher in the judgment day, and there would ensue a resurrection from the dead.[3]

Conversely, "In my vision at night I looked, and there before me was one like a son of man, coming with the clouds of heaven" (Dan. 7:13). He would come down rather than rise up to assume control, as the text elaborates: "He was given authority, glory and sovereign power."

Royal heir to David's throne or suffering servant? "Of the increase of his government and peace there will be no end. He will reign on David's throne and over his kingdom, establishing and upholding it with justice and righteousness from that time on and forever" (Isa. 9:7). God's oppressed people will be avenged and peace return to the land.

Conversely, "He was despised and rejected by men, a man of sorrows, and familiar with suffering" (Isa 53:3). (How dramatic a shift from royal sovereign to suffering servant!) "But he was pierced for our transgressions, he was crushed for our iniquities; the punishment that brought us peace was upon him, and by his wounds we are healed" (v. 5). Salvation will be achieved through his vicarious suffering.

The disciples were not immune from the pervasive Messianic ambiguity. When Jesus shared with them word of His impending death,

Peter would have none of it: "Never, Lord! This shall never happen to you!" (16:22). It must have appeared thoroughly out of keeping with a royal heir to the Davidic throne.

Thomas reacted quite differently to the prospect of Jesus' return to the Jerusalem environs and impending death. "Let us also go, that we may die with him," he implored the others (John 11:16). Was this simply an expression of "loyal despair" as some commentators assume, or perhaps because he viewed Jesus as the suffering servant? The latter appears a likely option.

We return to the response of the multitude. When the people witnessed the miraculous sign of feeding the crowd, they concluded: "Surely this is the Prophet who is to come" (John 6:14). Jesus, perceiving that they intended to compel Him to assume political rule, withdrew again to a deserted place. He had no intention of accommodating to their Messianic criteria.

At another time, John the Baptist sent his disciples to ask of Jesus: "Are you the one who was to come, or should we expect someone else?" (11:2). Jesus replied: "Go back and report to John what you hear and see. The blind receive sight, the lame walk, those who have leprosy are cured, the deaf hear, the dead are raised, and the good news is preached." His works should speak for themselves, and satisfy John's uncertainty.

After that, Jesus added: "Blessed is the man who does not fall away (take offense) on account of me." R.T. France appropriately comments:

> Many were "put off" by Jesus, when his style of ministry failed to tally with their expectations, and even offended against accepted conventions. "Good news to the poor" was an offence to the establishment, while a mission of the relief of suffering and the restoration of sinners would be at best irrelevant to those who fought for national liberation.[4]

The facts that seem to emerge are as follows. While ambiguity concerning the Messiah abounded, the popular focus was on his political role as deliverer. Seeing Jesus rejected this role, He chose to couch His Messianic claim in terms less misleading. When pressed, He was not reluctant to confirm His Messianic calling. Since Jesus often exhorted as God's Anointed, we turn first to consider this phenomenon.

Life Leverage

"Come, follow me." Only three words, they speak a volume. They characterize Jesus' Messianic appeal; all else resembles commentary.

Jesus repeated them more than once: at the calling of Peter and Andrew (4:19), in response to the disciple who requested first to bury his parents (8:22), when calling Matthew (9:9), and after admonishing a young man to sell all that he had and give to the needy (19:21). We may surmise that these are simply representative instances, recalling Jesus' customary practice.

Whether this may have been a formula shared with other rabbis of the time seems beside the point. Jesus uttered these words in the context of His Messianic mission. He bid others follow Him, not as one of many teachers but as the promised Prophet.

The implications were staggering. In military terms, He offered high ground not previously available.

The resulting contrast is worth exploring. For a time, Israel will be tried "in the furnace of affliction," but then restored to favor (Isa. 48:10; 49:8). For a time, Israel will be scattered to the winds, but then regathered. "The time is coming" when Yahweh will make a new covenant with His people, as He had previously done with those delivered from Egypt (cf. Jer. 31:31-32). The time then future was now!

Jesus assumed center stage with regard *to personal redemption*. He stood where we were unable to stand, thus to reconcile us to the Almighty.

Matthew provides a striking case in point. He was a tax collector who associated indiscriminately with "sinners" (9:11). The sinners (*'am ha'arez*, people of the land) were either unable or undisciplined to keep the finer provisions of the Torah. They were considered irreligious.

If for no other reason, Matthew assumed guilt by way of association. As we say with nod of approval: "Birds of a feather, flock together."

Were this not bad enough, Matthew compounded his guilt as a tax collector. While such were never popular, those of the time were especially despised. They were Jews who voluntarily hired out to the Romans. In addition, they often demanded excessive amounts to share with the Roman officials or increase their profits.

In the same breath, one might refer to the tax collector and heathen (18:17) or prostitute (21:32). People considered them an affront to God and a plague to society.

When Jesus saw Matthew sitting at his collector's booth, He invited him to "Follow me." What transpired must have come as a surprise to those looking on. Matthew immediately arose to follow Jesus. All that he had previously counted as gain, he gladly relinquished. All that might be demanded of him, he happily embraced.

While Jesus was having dinner at Matthew's house, many tax collectors and sinners joined in. When the Pharisees saw this, they inquired: "Why does your teacher eat with tax collectors and 'sinners'?" On hearing their question, Jesus replied: "It is not the healthy who need a doctor, but the sick. But go and learn what this means: 'I desire mercy, not sacrifice.' For I have not come to call the righteous, but sinners."

In a classic passage not dimmed by age, C.G. Montefiore reflects on what was at stake: "The Rabbis attached no less value to repentance than Jesus. They sang its praises and its efficacy in a thousand tones. They, too, urged that God cared more for the repentant than for the just who had never yielded to sin. They, too, welcomed the sinner in his repentance." Similarities aside,

> to seek out the sinner, and, instead of avoiding the bad companion, to choose him as your friend in order to work his moral redemption, this was, I fancy, something new in the religious history of Israel. ...It was, doubtless, often a daring method; even with Jesus it may not always have been successful. But it inaugurated a new idea: the idea of redemption, the idea of giving a fresh object of love and interest to the sinner, and so freeing him from his sin.[5]

"A daring method" no doubt, but no less realistic--given Jesus' Messianic leverage. He held the advantage of uniquely high ground.

Jesus' reference to the righteousness of the Pharisees was more than ironic. They were rigorous in their religious observance. Talmudic and Biblical writers agree that while some were hypocritical, others were not.

As for Jesus' disciples, they do not as a rule seem to share Matthew's dubious background. Peter and Andrew, as cases in point, appear as God-fearing people engaged in constructive enterprise. We must conclude that Jesus called persons indiscriminate of virtue to follow Him. Personal piety provides neither exception to nor substitute for Messianic salvation.

Jesus also took center stage *in redemptive history*. The Jews had looked forward to what Oscar Cullmann refers to as the "mid-point", between the "Present Age" and the "Age to Come". With Jesus, the mid-point had passed.

Cullmann likened this to "D-Day" and "V-Day", citing a World War II analogy. With Jesus, D-Day has occurred. He has established a firm beachhead. In time, V-Day will result. Rest assured, the invasion will successfully run its course.

As Paul would conclude: "In the past God overlooked such ignorance, but now he commands all people everywhere to repent" (Acts 17:30). The Messianic Age has dawned, and with it redemptive history has entered its final stage. Those who choose to reject Jesus are not only hopelessly dated but in serious danger.

One thing more needs to be considered. Jesus assumed center stage *in the redemption of creation.*

On one occasion, Jesus and His disciples were in a boat, when without warning, a storm broke with all its fury. Jesus was sleeping. The disciples went and woke Him, saying: "Lord save us! We're going to drown!" (8:25). He replied: "You of little faith, why are you so afraid?" Then He got up and rebuked the winds and the waves, and all was calm.

"The men" probably included others than the disciples. They were without exception amazed and asked: "What kind of man is this? Even the winds and the waves obey him!"

Jesus' stilling of the waves may be understood as an earnest for the restoration of all creation. It is not more, because "the whole creation has been groaning as in the pains of childbirth right up to the present time" (Rom. 8:22). It is not less, because the dramatic incident requires a satisfactory explanation. If not struck by the awesome character of Jesus' authority over creation, we have as yet to take the text seriously.

Only some loose ends remain to be tied up. Jesus on occasion employs the abbreviated exhortation: "Come to me," or simply: "Come." *"Come to me,* all you who are weary and burdened, and I will give you rest. Take my yoke upon you and learn from me, for I am gentle and humble of heart, and you will find rest for your souls. For my yoke is easy and my burden is light" (11:28-30).

The expression appears similar to that of Ben Sira, who held that the study of Torah brought him rest (Sir. 51:27-29). Even so, the spirit is quite different. Gentleness and humility characterize Jesus' yoke; not strict obedience to stated precepts. Its thrust more resembles the admonition: "Let go and let God!"

More to the point, Jesus tacks by way of His Messianic authority. His yoke takes precedence over all else.

On another occasion, the disciples saw Jesus walking on the lake and thought it an apparition. "Take courage!" Jesus called out. "It is I. Don't be afraid" (14:27). "Lord, if it's you," Peter replied, "tell me to come to you on the water."

"Come," Jesus said. Peter set out to obey, but when he saw the wind churning the waves, he was afraid and began to sink. "Lord, save me!" he cried out. Immediately Jesus reached out His hand, and caught him.

"You of little faith," Jesus addressed His disciple, "why did you doubt?" Jesus and Peter climbed into the boat and the water calmed.

These and similar expressions were meant to encourage. In one instance, Jesus admonished the paralytic: "Take heart, son; your sins are forgiven" (9:2). In another, He assured the woman who had suffered for twelve years: "Take heart, daughter, your faith has healed you" (9:22).

Jesus calls for trust. He offered the disciples no detailed prospect for what the future would hold. It was enough that He would be with them and for them.

One day at a time, one step at a time. This was and is the character of a life as lived by faith.

It requires obedience. We hear Jesus bid us come. We hear Him tell us go. We hear Him urge us to pray. We hear Him encourage us to forgive. We cannot negotiate a response. We can only obey or walk away.

Discipleship is costly. "Teacher, I will follow you wherever you go" (8:19). Jesus replied: "Foxes have holes and birds of the air have nests, but the Son of Man has no place to lay his head." Jesus was no typical rabbi, nor following Him a slight matter.

"Lord, first let me go and bury my father," the scribe responded. Matthew does not record the context.

> If his father was already dead, his request was a natural, even essential, one. The dead must be buried within 24 hours, and the duty was incumbent on the son. It was so important that it took precedence over essentially religious duties (Berakoth 3:1), and even justified priests in contracting defilement (Lv. 23:2).[6]

If, on the other hand, the father was not dead, the request amounted to an indefinite postponement. This seems the more likely explanation.

Jesus addressed His disciples: "If anyone would come after me, he must deny himself and take up his cross and follow me" (16:24). The first two imperatives (deny, take up) are aorist tense, suggesting finality, the third (follow) present tense, implying response and continued faithfulness.

To take up one's cross recalls the practice of bearing the crossbar to the place of execution, and experiencing the taunts of those along the way. The disciples had to realize that this might literally occur. As Bonhoeffer put the matter: "When Christ calls a man, He bids him come and die."

Death, never less! All on the altar of sacrifice, never part! Wherever He leads, never on a selective basis! Jesus solemnly adds: "For whoever wants to save his life will lose it, but whoever loses his life for me will find it" (16:25).

When drawing similarities between Jesus' teaching and that of others, we muddy the water. As the Anointed of God, He was unique, as were His exhortations so understood. They require that we lay aside not only the evil but good to serve the ultimate.

Such principles as Jesus may set forth, He does so in narrative context. The latter is critical to understanding the former. We must turn back time and again to the Biblical text to seek guidance for our pilgrim journey. We need to hear the admonitions of Jesus, spoken in concrete situations, addressed to our ever changing experience. They are ever old and ever new.

Those who have decided to follow Jesus, will listen for the Messianic drum beat and pick up on its cadence. The clamor of the world fades away in the distance.

Chapter 3

THE KINGDOM OF HEAVEN (GOD)

As previously mentioned, Jesus came preaching: "Repent, the kingdom of heaven is near" (4:17). Matthew employs the kingdom of heaven instead of God in all but four instances: 12:28, 19:24, 21:31, and 21:43. In contrast, he employs the kingdom of heaven on thirty-four occasions. This "appears to reflect the characteristic Jewish tendency to refer to God only indirectly or by circumlocution."[7] Persons substituted it out of deference to the sanctity of God's name.

There seems to have been sufficient common ground between Jesus' understanding of the kingdom and that of His listeners to allow for subsequent refinement. Those assembled also were vitally interested in the topic. They chafed under Roman occupation, and longed for deliverance.

The Kingdom Message

The kingdom of heaven solicits images of God's rule. It is in perpetuity--seeing God is ever sovereign, uniquely present with the advent of the Messianic Age, and future concerning the consummation of history.

The kingdom is in perpetuity. The psalmist describes a time when the kings of the earth take their stand against the Lord and His Anointed. "Let us break their chains," they agree, "and throw off their fetters" (2:4). Then, "the One enthroned in heaven" laughs at their presumption, and scoffs at their fruitless endeavor. They constitute no threat to His perpetual reign.

On another occasion, King Nebuchadnezzar mused as he was walking on the roof of his royal palace: "Is not this the great Babylon I have built as the royal residence, by my mighty power and for the glory of my majesty?" (Dan. 4:27). While the words were still on his lips, "a voice came from heaven" announcing that his authority would be taken from him, and he would live as the wild animals until he came to acknowledge "that the Most High is sovereign over the kingdoms of men and gives them to anyone he wishes."

Immediately what was promised came to pass. "He was driven away from people and ate grass like cattle. His body was drenched with the dew of heaven until his hair grew like the feathers of an eagle and his nails like the claws of a bird." When at last he came to his senses, the king honored and glorified the Most High with the witness: "His dominion is an eternal dominion; his kingdom endures from generation to generation" (v. 34).

"How awesome is the Lord Most High, the great King over all the earth!" (Psa. 47:2). Such was the Hebrew legacy concerning the kingdom.

The rule of God became especially associated with Israel, in keeping with her Covenant. This was fashioned after a vassal treaty, promising blessing in turn for obedience. "I will walk among you and be your God, and you will be my people" (Lev. 26:12).

This would serve also as a reminder to the nations of God's rightful rule. "Come near, you nations, and listen; pay attention, you peoples!" (Isa. 34:1). Do not underestimate the wrath of God, nor His compassion for those who repent.

"Throughout the course of human history, God exercised his sovereignty through his Law. Anyone who submits to the Law thereby submits himself to the reign of God."[8] The principle was applicable, whether to Hebrew or Gentile, whether with Mosaic or Noahic Covenant.

"Indeed, when Gentiles, who do not have the law, do by nature things required by the law, they are a law for themselves" (Rom. 2:14). For it is not those who hear but abide by the teaching who are righteous in God's sight.

With the passing of time, the kingdom came increasingly to take on a nationalistic character. The nations were faulted for substituting their patron deities for the Most High. As for the Hebrews, they struggled with varying degrees of success.

The northern kingdom was least effective. Jeroboam set up rival sanctuaries at Bethel and Dan, built shrines on the high places, and consecrated priests without consideration to lineage. His successors perpetuated his heretical ways.

The southern kingdom experienced revival from time to time, as with

Hezekiah and Josiah. Even so, these simply postponed the inevitable. Jerusalem fell before the onslaught of the Babylonians. The land lay desolate and many people carried off into captivity.

Hope did not perish in the ashes of the Holy City. The faithful still anticipated the coming of the Messiah to reassert the kingdom prerogatives. It was in this context that the disciples asked of Jesus: "Lord, are you at this time going to restore the kingdom to Israel?" (Acts 1:6). The imperfect tense implies that it was a recurring question.

The disciples had already experienced an earnest of the kingdom. "But if I drive out demons by the Spirit of God," Jesus observed, "then the kingdom is come upon you" (Matt. 12:28). Matthew's use here of the kingdom of God instead of heaven, serves to contrast with the kingdom of Satan. "Jesus thus claims the arrival in his ministry of that to which the Old Testament and Judaism had looked forward. It is already present, but its character is not that of popular expectation; it is a spiritual victory, not a national or political one--the enemy is Satan, not Rome."[9] The Pharisees were not alone in failing to grasp the implications; the disciples also struggled to get the matter into proper focus.

As evidence of the kingdom being present, Jesus cast out demons, healed the infirm, stilled the tempest, and declared good news. It was as if heaven touched down wherever He went.

"All authority in heaven and on earth has been given to me," Jesus prefaced His kingdom mandate. "Therefore go and make disciples of all nations, baptizing them in the name of the Father and of the Son and of the Holy Spirit, and teaching them to obey everything I have commanded you" (28:19-20).

They were first to tarry until baptized with the Holy Spirit, as John had promised: "I baptize you with water for repentance. But after me will come one who is more powerful than I, whose sandals I am not fit to carry. He will baptize with the Holy Spirit and with fire" (3:11-12).

> Jesus looked upon his disciples as the nucleus of Israel who accepted his proclamation of the kingdom of God and who, therefore, formed the true people of God, the spiritual Israel. He indicated his purpose to bring into being his ekklesia who would recognize his messiahship and be the people of the Kingdom and at the same time the instrument of the Kingdom in the world.[10]

The church was not the kingdom, but resulted from and was the particular instrument of the kingdom.

In a more extended sense, the kingdom remained future. Jesus had this in mind when He commented: "No one knows about that day or hour, not the angels in heaven, nor the Son, but only the Father" (24:36). It will come when unexpected, with persons carrying on as usual, as before the deluge of Noah's time.

There will be false prophets claiming to be the Christ, and deceiving many. There will be wars and rumors of wars. There will be persecution and martyrdom. There will be an increase of wickedness, and a decrease of ardor. "And this gospel of the kingdom will be preached in the whole world as a testimony to all nations, and then the end will come" (24:14).

The disciples were to live toward the future, in recognition that they must give account of what they had done with their opportunities. They were to live toward the future, knowing that to serve the least of Jesus' brothers was as if serving Him (25:40). They were to live toward the future, anticipating that the suffering of the present is little compared to the glory as yet to be revealed.

Ben Viviano cogently summarizes: "The kingdom of God as proclaimed by Jesus may be described as social, political, personalistic (respectful of individual freedom), universal in intent, transcendent in origin, earthly in realization, present in sign, future in fullness."[11] It certainly bears repeating: "present in sign and future in fullness."

Kingdom Concerns

Jesus, echoing the message of John the Baptist, urged the multitude to repent in preparation for the approaching kingdom. They used identical wording: "Repent, for the kingdom of heaven is near" (3:1; 4:17).

Repentance comes first, without which we can not hope to experience the rich benefits of the kingdom. Sorrow plays a part, sorrow for having done wrong and failing to do right.

There is more. Repentance implies what some have called *Godly sorrow*, implying the intent to turn from sin. It involves an about-face.

In this connection, Judas stands in vivid contrast to Peter. The former was "seized with remorse," so much so that he took his life (27:1-5). Conversely, Peter "went outside and wept bitterly," after which he became a fearless leader of the apostolic community. One bore his sorrow to the grave, while the other refined it into profitable ministry.

Genuine repentance bears fruit. When John observed many Pharisees and Sadducees among those coming to be baptized, he rebuked them: "You brood of vipers. Who warned you to flee from the coming wrath? Produce fruit in keeping with repentance" (3:7-8).

The notion of fruit plays an important role in Matthew's account. Jesus warned of false prophets with the observation: "By their fruit you will recognize them" (7:16). Later He commented: "Make a tree good and its fruit will be good, or make a tree bad and its fruit will be bad, for a tree is recognized by its fruit" (12:33). Still later, Jesus announced: "I tell you that the kingdom of God will be taken away from you and given to a people who will produce its fruit" (21:43).

It was a message suited to the time. The designation "kingdom of God" (rather than heaven) in this instance seems to emphasize God's saving presence with His people. The kingdom would be transferred from those who presumed on God's grace without being transformed by it to others happy to pick up crumbs from God's festive table. The latter would be made up of Hebrews and Gentiles alike, without respect to ethnic considerations.

It was also a message for all times. We do not preach grace in competition with works, but a grace that generates works. As James put it: "Show me your faith without deeds, and I will show you my faith by what I do" (2:18).

Faith is nonetheless the means by which we appropriate God's promises. We respond to Jesus' exhortation to repent and reset our course. We press on trusting that His grace is sufficient to meet our every challenge. We succeed because He continues with us "always, to the very end of the age" (28:20).

We will digress at this point to consider a related exhortation. Jesus admonished: "Be perfect, as your heavenly father is perfect" (5:48). The perfection to which Jesus refers must be understood in context: if we show courtesy only to our friends, that is altogether ordinary. If we would be *perfect*, we must extend our concern to all despite of qualifications.

Jesus also instructed a young man that if he would inherit eternal life, he should sell his possessions and give to the poor (19:21). If we would be perfect, we must press beyond legalistic observance to embrace loving service.

Considering such demands, the disciples concluded that it would be better not to marry (19:10). They reasoned that if the best were unattainable, one should not settle for what approximates it. They were in error, as Jesus went on to point out.

Some, Jesus observed, were incapable of marriage from birth. Others were castrated, such as those who had the responsibility of guarding royal harems or certain cultic priests. Still others voluntarily renounced marriage "because of the kingdom of heaven." Each ought to perfect the manner in which he/she is called, making the most of the opportunities that it affords.

Leonhard Goppelt succinctly sums up:

> Each of Jesus' demands was after nothing less than a transformation of the person from the very core, i.e., total repentance. When we inquire if people were mentioned in the Jesus tradition who realized his commandments then we quickly discover that Jesus' commandment was lived only by Jesus himself.[12]

Though others fall short, they are expected to pick themselves up, brush themselves off, and continue. As far as Jesus' calling is concerned, it is always too soon for us to quit.

Turning to a related concern, Jesus not only admonished persons to repent but "seek first his (God's) kingdom and his righteousness" (6:33). If we prioritize the kingdom, other concerns will fall into place. If we fail to do so, nothing will turn out right.

Righteousness resembles an investment in eternity. It also contributes to a full and rewarding life. The righteous stand to gain whether in life or through death. God is no person's debtor.

Jesus told parables with the kingdom priority in view. It seems that when a man discovered a treasure, he sold all that he had to purchase the field where the treasure was found (13:44). In like manner, a merchant sold all that he had to purchase a pearl of great value (13:45-46).

To seek first the kingdom means earnestly to search out God's will and do it. Some do not care to search. They are more comfortable not knowing what God would have them do.

Others are merely curious. They like to discover God's will not in order obey it, but simply for the sake of knowing. They are no more to be commended than the previous folk.

We must resist social pressure. Jesus urgently plead: "Enter through the narrow gate. For wide is the gate and broad is the road that leads to destruction, and many enter through it. But small is the gate and narrow the road that leads to life, and only a few find it" (7:13-14).

The gate is narrowed as the result of the costly demands of discipleship, most notably with persecution. As Jesus put it in another kingdom parable: "The one who received the seed that fell on rocky places is the man who hears the word and at once receives it with joy. But since he has no root, he lasts only a short time. When trouble or persecution comes because of the word, he quickly falls away" (20:21).

Along a somewhat different line, Jesus urged: "Let the little children come to me, and do not hinder them, for the kingdom of heaven belongs to such as these" (19:14). He had observed earlier on: "Unless you change and become like little children, you will never enter the kingdom of heaven" (18:3).

> When Jesus called a "little child" over to him and put the little child in their midst, he gave substance to what he was about to teach. ...Unless the disciples exhibit a childlike indifference to greatness by the world's standards, they cannot (the double negative in Greek emphasizes this) expect to "enter the kingdom of heaven."[13]

There was no way that they could gain entrance, let alone excel, unless they would exchange their striving for position for God's benediction on the humble.

Some will be surprised with their lot. Jesus warned the chief priests and elders: "I tell you the truth, the tax-collectors and the prostitutes are entering the kingdom of God ahead of you" (21:31). John came preaching the way of righteousness, but you did not believe him. Even when the tax-collectors and prostitutes believed, you did not repent and believe.

Seven times Jesus pronounced woe on His Pharisaic adversaries (23:13,15,16,23,25,27,29). There seems no convincing reason to suppose these scathing rebukes are not authentic. While not necessary to suppose that all scribes and Pharisees were implicated, the self-seeking and hypocritical attitudes Jesus assails were all too evident in the hostility building to His crucifixion.

Repent-believe, give the kingdom matters priority, and do not in any way inhibit others. These appear as Jesus' prime concerns in kingdom perspective, whether now or in preparation for the future.

We cannot frustrate God's purposes in any case. It is better that we learn to cooperate, with its resulting benefits. Such seems to be Jesus' rationale as derived from His kingdom exhortations.

Chapter 4

THE SCRIPTURES

The *Torah* (teaching, law) was thought to be handed down from Mosaic times, through the prophets, and in the writings. Increased emphasis was placed on oral tradition, which would eventually become codified in the Talmud. Persons speculated on how the advent of Messiah would alter the existing situation. No one thought for a moment that Torah would be repudiated. On the contrary, it would be exalted to its rightful place, and come to permeate life thoroughly. One would not be far off target to describe the coming era as "The Golden Age of Torah".

Jesus denied the charge that He would subvert the teaching. He lived the Torah life and encouraged others to do so. He also demanded that controversy be resolved in accordance with that written. He tenaciously resisted religious casuistry, pressing instead for original intent. There was not even a hint of lawlessness in His demeanor or instruction.

Posturing

Jesus set about to position Himself related to the Torah. "Do not think that I have come to abolish the Law and the Prophets," He announced; "I have not come to abolish them but to fulfill them" (5:17). The passage is, as we shall see, plagued with ambiguities.

While commentators tend to pass over the phrase "I am come" with little concern, there may be more to this than meets the eye. What Donald Guthrie points out regarding John's gospel may apply in more muted fashion to the synoptics:

> "I" adds particular dignity to the statements of Jesus. It is remarkable that

this use does not sound audacious on the lips of Jesus. What would be presumptuous in others appears natural to him. But the very frequency of the "I" draws attention to his own person in a striking way, which prepares the reader for the more specific "I am" sayings.[14]

We turn to the "I am" revelation of God to Moses from the burning bush (Exod. 3:14), and work our way from there. While the designation could mean several things, it probably accents God's faithfulness through subsequent generations. He would be known in the course of redemptive history.

This evokes Paul's succinct conclusion: "God was reconciling the world to himself in Christ" (2 Cor. 5:19). It was for this reason that He had come.

As for posturing, "I am come" falls between Jesus' confession "I am" (witnessing to His incarnate character), and I am metaphors (suggesting His unique ministries). Illustrative of the last, Jesus was described as "the bread of life" and "the light of the world." "I am come" implies continuity with God's previous redemptive efforts, and boldly embodies the present.

We have laid a foundation, but must build upon it. Jesus assured everyone within hearing that He had not come to abolish Torah but fulfill it. If we successfully address the latter, it will take care of the former.

Three plausible interpretations come to mind. On one occasion, certain Pharisees and scribes questioned Jesus: "Why do your disciples break the tradition of the elders? They don't wash their hands before they eat!" (15:2). Had Jesus encouraged them to disregard Torah?

Jesus turned matters around: "And why do you break the command of God for the sake of your tradition?" "For God said" honor your father and mother, implying (among other things) that we care for them in their need. "But you say" that we can void the responsibility by devoting our gifts to God. "Thus you nullify the word of God with your tradition." While bent on nitpicking, they had blatantly disregarded the more critical matters.

Another possibility presents itself. Since Matthew regularly uses the verb *plerosai* (to fulfill) concerning prophecy, perhaps Jesus meant bring to pass what the prophets had promised. He would keep God's commitment.

The temptation account thus could be understood. When tempted, Jesus confidently replied: "It is written." Fortified with the Word of God, He stoutly resisted the adversary's effort to derail His mission.

An additional alternative needs to be considered.

The verb can and frequently does convey the meaning "to clarify the true meaning of" something. Certainly it can be argued that what Jesus is doing in this legal material of Matt v-vii is trying to restore the original meaning of the Law where this seemed to be obscured by the accretions of commentary.[15]

On another occasion, Jesus was commenting on the binding character of marriage (19:4-6). Certain of the Pharisees put Him to the test: "Why then did Moses command that a man give his wife a certificate of divorce and send her away?" Jesus replied that Moses permitted divorce because "your hearts were hard," but "it was not so from the beginning." The point is that what God has joined, we ought not to separate.

We do not necessarily have to decide among these options. "Some combination of the above" or "all of the above" may be the preferred answer.

Consider that ambiguity often served Jesus' purpose. By way of example, the disciples asked Jesus: "Why do you speak to the people in parables?" (13:10). He replied that it was so that those who have might be given more. That is, the disciples could enhance their knowledge through their present understanding. As for "the people", the light would have to dawn more gradually and with greater uncertainty.

Jesus in countless other ways meant to position Himself as a firm advocate of the Torah. When misunderstood, He affirmed His commitment. When criticized, He demanded that Torah arbitrate. When confronted with obstinacy, He called for Torah fidelity. Jesus' Torah-related exhortations are an important component to His ethical instruction.

Taking Stock

"It is written" was Jesus' preferred formula for referring to the scriptures. He used it three times during His temptation (4:4,7,10), again when cleansing the temple (21:13), and still again to account for His disciples falling away (26:31). In the two first settings, He placed the emphasis on voluntary compliance, the third on known result.

Jesus thus reminds us of God's sovereign will, test it though we may. C.S. Lewis reasoned that God relates to us as sons or tools, the difference being that the former deliberately seeks to cooperate. In the end, all serve God's purposes regardless of disposition.

Time and circumstances will not alter the conditions. "I tell you the truth, until heaven and earth disappear, not the smallest letter, not the least stroke of the pen, will by any means disappear from the Law until everything is accomplished" (5:18). Trust and obey, there is no other way to measure up to Jesus' high regard for Holy Writ.

Closely related to the foregoing, there are variations on the question: "Have you not read?" These include references to the original intent of marriage (19:4), praise ordained from the mouths of children and infants (21:16), and the stone rejected becoming the capstone (21:42).

They combine to stress the abiding relevance of Biblical teaching. This implies that we are responsible to seek out truth, and that our failure to do so leaves us without excuse. Otherwise stated, we are responsible not only for what we know but have the possibility of knowing.

Sometimes Jesus probed for a deeper meaning, not immediately evident to those listening. Thus, when criticized by some for having table fellowship with sinners, He admonished them to weigh the significance of the text: "I desire mercy, not sacrifice" (9:13; cf. Hos. 6:6). So also he charged those attempting to trap him: "You are in error because you do not know the Scriptures or the power of God" (22:27). That is, you fail to consider the differences between this life and that yet future.

These remind us that we must consider the teaching with care. Otherwise, we will end hearing only what we want to hear rather than what we need to hear. We also reach false conclusions based on partial evidence.

Jesus especially accented the importance of keeping the commandments. Illustrative, a rich man approached Him with the question: "Teacher, what good thing must I do to get eternal life?" (19:16). Jesus called into question the person's presuppositions.

> If Jesus is simply *Teacher*, then he is calculated to know no more and no less than any other teacher as to what actions are deemed "good for" entrance into the age-to-come. If he is *Good Teacher* (as in Mark and Luke), then Jesus will not allow the questioner to use the word or ascription lightly.[16]

"Good" relates essentially to character, and only God is ultimately good. God's goodness is expressed by the commandments, the keeping of which reflects man's goodness. Jesus responded: "If you want to enter life, obey the commandments."

"Which?" the man wanted to know. Perhaps he meant to hedge. "Do not murder," Jesus replied, exhorting him to faithful observance. So also do not commit adultery, steal, or give false testimony. Honor your father and mother, and love your neighbor as yourself.

The questioner breathed a sigh of relief. "All these I have kept," he confided with perhaps a touch of pride. "What do I still lack?" "If you want to be perfect, go, sell your possessions and give to the poor, and you will have treasure in heaven. Then come, follow me." The man went away sad, because he had great wealth that he was not willing to relinquish. Jesus used the occasion to point how difficult it becomes for a rich person to enter the kingdom of God.

Sometime later, a scribe asked of Jesus: "Teacher, which is the greatest commandment in the Law?" (22:36). In a manner of speaking, he wanted to know the bottom line. This was a question that would continue to solicit rabbinic speculation. Rabbi Akiva suggested that it was to love our neighbor as ourself. Rabbi Simeon said that it was to recognize oneself as created in God's image. Rabbi Simlai, taking Amos 5:4 as his proof-text, concluded it was to seek God and live.

Jesus replied: "Love the Lord your God with all your heart and with all your soul and with all your mind." This is the first and greatest commandment. The second is like it: "Love your neighbor as yourself. On these hang all the Law and Prophets. "Obey these," Jesus admonished all who would hear. At this point, He had reached the crux of the matter, but had something important to add.

A distinctive set of exhortations involves some form of "you have heard it said," followed shortly after that with "but I tell you" (5:21-22,27-28,31-32,33-34,38-39,43-44). While a variant of "I say to you" is common in Matthew (58 times, compared to only 14 in Mark and 45 in Luke), it occurs with "you have heard it said" only in this extended passage.

We will look at these six antitheses first as a whole and then separately. Two options are available to us: either Jesus means to contrast His teaching with Torah as such, or to other interpretation of it. Since we have excluded the former, it leaves us with the latter. We also understand Jesus' teaching as normative for the present as well as future.

It has been said that we ought not to commit murder, and those who do so will be brought to judgment. Upon which, Jesus declares that God finds reprehensible the anger that causes violence and the taking of life.

Jewish commentators have been quick to point out that there is nothing especially novel in this antithesis. Rabbinic precedent is not lacking. In fact, Matthew does not seem especially concerned with the novelty of Jesus' admonitions, but how He applied Torah to human relationships. Thus even when anger has not run its course to murder, it was thoroughly destructive to the fragile character of life together.

It has been said that we should not commit adultery, but "I tell you that anyone who looks at a woman lustfully has already committed adultery with her in his heart." Seeing that lust when given opportunity results in the act of adultery, lust is in disposition already adultery.

In rabbinic literature, this takes a bizarre turn with the "bloodied Pharisee," who attempting not to look at a beautiful woman runs into a wall--injuring himself. Conversely, Jesus meant to distinguish between looking and "looking lustfully."

It has been said that if a man divorce his wife, he must give her a certificate (cf. Deut. 24:1). Divorce is not commanded, but recognized and regulated. Jesus excavates below the level of regulation, to come up with the intent of marriage. God meant for monogamous union instead of serial polygamy.

Jesus' words are not expressly directed toward the phenomenon of fractured marriages. Such obviously occur, in spite of the ideal and good intentions. It appears consistent with the thrust of the passage to suppose that such would be dealt with sensitively, supportively, and with the highest regard for divine intent.

It has been said that we should qualify our taking of oaths, but Jesus declared that our word should be our bond. Jesus thus invalidates rampant casuistry, which distinguishes between binding and nonbinding oaths. By certifying one's word by appeal to heaven, earth, Jerusalem, or one's head drains credibility from a professed commitment to truth.

John Calvin observed that a lie is any attempt to conceal the truth. We ought rather to strive to tell the truth in love. Not to hurt others or disgrace them, but rather out of concern for their best interests.

It has been said "an eye for an eye." The law of *talion* was intended to set proper limits on retaliation and compensation. Let the punishment fit the crime.

Jesus labored the point that we ought not to allow what another person has done to us influence how we behave toward him. Do not demand just compensation as a condition for concern. Be prepared to go the second mile. Bear in mind God's longsuffering with us.

It has been said that we should love our neighbor, and hate our enemy. Jesus admonishes that we love our enemies, and pray for those who persecute us.

This final antithesis provides a fitting conclusion to the passage. It was love of one's enemies that fired the imagination of the early Christian missionaries and martyrs, and caused others to marvel at them. This was the unassailable apologetic for the Christian faith.

It also calls our attention back to Jesus' introductory comment on surpassing righteousness (5:20). In that His exhortations press beyond outward conformity to inner compatibility, they surpass the righteousness of the Pharisees and scribes. Ought we to view this higher righteousness in a quantitative or qualitative sense? Likely both.

The quantitative comparison is obvious anyhow. The one must surpass the other.

Ulrich Luz is not content to leave the matter in those terms.

> The higher righteousness of the disciples is not only a quantitative increase of the fulfilling of the law--measured on the Torah--but primarily a qualitative intensification of the life before God--measured by love. Verse 20 stands, so to speak, in the middle between these two conceptions, dependent on whether it is read "from the front" or "from the back."[17]

Love provides the needed dynamic for doing good, and cultivates creative means to accomplish that purpose. Paul extolled among its virtues: "Love is patient, love is kind, it does not envy, it does not boast, it is not proud. It is not rude, it is not self-seeking, it is not easily angered, it keeps no record of wrongs. Love does not delight in evil but rejoices with the truth. It always protects, always trusts, always hopes, always perseveres" (1 Cor. 13:4-7). Jesus exhorts us to love and obey, for in loving we obey.

Chapter 5

THE COMMUNITY

As noted earlier, when Jesus saw the crowds, he went up on a mountainside. Gathering the disciples, He began to instruct them. In response to the call of Jesus, they had *ipso facto* entered upon life together.

These disciples would prove to be a diverse lot. They came to differ regarding all those things that the world thinks important: ethnic and racial character, economic and social status, age and gender. They would have in common what the world tragically views as inconsequential, a common commitment to Christ.

Believers Together

The disciples did not learn of fellowship in the abstract, but as they jostled about following Jesus. They could compare the circumstances in which they were called, their experience of being called, and what had subsequently come to pass from their calling. Each day and each event contributed to their understanding and appreciation of life in Christ and as community.

Matthew mentions the church as such only twice: once concerning its foundation (16:18), the other with discipline (18:17). They are nonetheless instructive.

A nearly vertical rock outcropping, with grotto from which courses a steady flow of water, dominates the region of Caesarea Phillipi. Near to the ruins of the ancient village, it likely solicited Jesus' comment concerning the rock on which He would build His church.

Matthew records a private gathering, in a non-Jewish setting, with the Galilean multitudes absent. It comes as a climax to an extended section beginning with 4:17, related to Jesus' Galilean ministry. It anticipates His turning toward Jerusalem, and the passion account.

Jesus probed His disciples with the question: "Who do people say the Son of Man is?" (6:13). They replied: "Some say John the Baptist, and still others, Jeremiah or one of the prophets." That is, there was a consensus that the Son of Man would be in the prophetic tradition. Perhaps John the Baptist or Jeremiah, since they were associated with the call to repentance.

"But what about you?" Jesus pressed them. How does your view differ from that of the multitudes? More to the point, "Who do you say I am?"

Simon Peter was seldom at a loss for words: "You are the Christ, the Son of the living God." Given the article, Simon means to identify Jesus as the one-as-yet-to-come. He had come in fulfillment of Israel's hopes and after countless frustrations. The latter designation would most likely be an allusion to a prominent Messianic text: "You are my Son, ...and I will make the nations your inheritance" (Psa. 2:7-8).

The Master was quick to respond: "Blessed are you, Simon son of Jonah, for this was not revealed by man, but by my Father in heaven." Whereas Simon had witnessed to Jesus as the Son of the living God, Jesus in turn referred to Simon as the son of Jonah--perhaps referring to the prophet by that name. The truth which Simon declared, he spoke as would a prophet coached by God.

Jesus continued speaking: "And I tell you that you are Peter, and on this rock I will build my church." "The crucial question is the identity of the 'rock' on which the church is to be founded. Jesus' statement involves a wordplay between *petros* (an isolated rock or stone) and *petra* (a rock ledge).[18] Even without a firsthand knowledge of the setting, it would appear that Jesus intended a play on words. With reconstruction, we could imagine that Jesus likened Simon to one of the stones that lined the bottom of the stream, as over against the sheer rock cliff rising overhead.

Unfortunately, the waters were muddied (pun intended) by denominational controversy over the claim to Papal primacy, which has no direct bearing on the text. Paul comments as follows: "For no one can lay any foundation other than the one already laid, which is Jesus Christ" (1 Cor. 3:11). In context, it seems obvious that he makes reference to the church by way of a common tradition.

Jesus adds that "the gates of hades" will not prevail against His church. If we assume the gates of hades should be taken as synonymous with "the gates of death" (cf. Psa. 9:13), this would suggest that the church will survive despite every attempt to do it in. Speculation about the church successfully storming the fortification of evil or overcoming its strategy, as contrived in the gate rooms, while possible appear somewhat strained.

The emphatic use of the first person needs to be considered in passing. Peter has witnessed to Jesus being the Christ, and Jesus was about to acknowledge the claim as true. As the Anointed One, "I" tell you that you are a stone, but "I" will build my church instead on this ledge. "I" will also give you the keys of the kingdom, so that what is bound on earth will be bound in heaven, and loosed on earth will be loosed in heaven.

> *Shall be bound and shall be loosed* are literally future perfects ("shall have been bound" and "shall have been loosed"), and as the future perfect sounds as stilted in Greek as in English, the tense is apparently deliberate. In that case it is not that heaven will ratify Peter's independent decisions, but that Peter will pass on decisions that have already been made in heaven.[19]

They are, as it were, still Jesus' keys.

"To bind" and "to loose" are technical terms in rabbinic usage meaning "to forbid" and "to permit". They are used here and in 18:18 concerning the task of reconciliation. It is in the latter connection that Matthew refers again to the church.

"If your brother sins," not necessarily "against you" (a problematic addition), you are responsible to bring it to his attention. If that does not clear up the problem, you should enlist the help of one or two witnesses, not simply or primarily to establish guilt but to resolve the problem. If this fails, "tell the matter to the church," and if he refuses "to listen even to the church," treat him as an outsider.

We discover the same three-stage procedure in Qumran legislation (1QS 5:25-6:1). Attempts at reconciliation should begin one on one, proceed by involving as few as possible, and as the last resort to the corporate fellowship. We should not allow problems to fester, infect the body, and disrupt its ministry.

We err if we suppose that Jesus' concern for the church were restricted to these two select instances. While seldom explicit, the church as community is everywhere implicit. So we concluded earlier concerning Jesus' calling out the disciples from the multitude. So Jesus assures us by taking the disciples aside to instruct them in the truth more perfectly. So can we gather from His wish to institute a memorial meal with them. So can we conclude from His mandate that they disciple all nations.

Still more critical for the present topic, "the special ethical demands made on the disciples presuppose a community."[20] Jesus pointed the disciples to righteousness that surpassed, quantitatively and qualitatively, that commonly embraced as the norm. This was not (as some have assumed) an interim ethic, but a challenge consistent with kingdom leverage.

Taking all the above into consideration, it would be surprising if Jesus had not exhorted His disciples concerning life together. They were to realize their calling in community.

Guidelines

Jesus does not admonish the community to give alms, pray, and fast, but how they should do so. These three acts of religious devotion have been fundamental to Jewish piety over the years. Conversely, they are not always properly motivated.

"When you give to the needy," do not do it to be honored of men (6:1-2). "And when you pray," do not do it to be seen of men (v. 5). "When you fast," do not call attention to it (v. 6). Religious devotion should honor God instead of seeking the acclaim of men.

Those who seek the praise of others should expect nothing else. They store up their treasures on earth, where "moth and rust destroy," rather than secure in heaven.

"But when you give to the needy, do not let your left hand know what your right hand is doing" (6:3).

> The general sense is plain. But does the left hand stand for a man's best friend (as still in modern Arabic), so that not even he is supposed to know? Or do we have a figurative command that a disciple should not let himself think about his deeds of charity? Probably the expression is to be understood literally, a gift should be slipped unobtrusively to the receiver with the right hand alone, not offered with both hands in a fashion designed to attract the attention of others nearby.[21]

Jesus abruptly concluded: "Then your Father, who sees what is done in secret, will reward you." Some find this saying troubling, fearing it amounts to *quid pro quo* (something for something). This is not the case with closer scrutiny. Jesus admonishes not because of the reward as such, but out of religious devotion.

It may be further noted that the reward need not be in kind. C.S. Lewis graphically illustrated this fact by telling a story of those in hell deciding to enjoy a picnic in heaven. They had hardly arrived before beginning to complain, and were anxious to get back where they had come from. The pleasures of heaven were not at all like what they had imagined.

Jesus shifted His focus to prayer. Do not pray standing in the synagogue or on the street corner. Prayer in the synagogue was led by one chosen for that purpose. If chosen, one should appreciatively and humbly embrace the opportunity. He ought not use the occasion for ostentation.

Persons would not as a rule pray on a street corner.

> In the morning and in the evening the devout Jew would recite the Shema (three short passages of Scripture from Deuteronomy 6 and 11 and Numbers 15), and at nine in the morning, noon, and three in the afternoon he would go through the Shemoneh Esreh (the Eighteen Benedictions). Acts 3:1 notes that Peter and John went to the temple "at the time of prayer--at three in the afternoon." According to Jewish custom, if you were in the streets at this time it was proper to stop, turn toward the temple, and pray (cf. the Moslem practice even today).[22]

One should not plan that this happen as a way of displaying his religious zeal.

Do not babbel on as the pagans are prone to do. They think that prayer has efficacy in and of itself. They suppose that there is merit to lengthy prayer. Neither is true. Prayer serves only as it expresses communion with God. Lengthy prayer may prove unnecessary, seeing God already knows our every need.

"This, then, is how you ought to pray," Jesus exhorts by way of example. What follows would better be described, not as *The Lord's Prayer*, but as *The Disciples' Prayer*. The concerns expressed are corporate: being addressed to *our* Father, for *our* daily bread, to forgive us *our* trespasses as we have forgiven those who trespassed against us, and lead *us* not into temptation but deliver *us* from the evil one.

The prayer comes across as similar to Jewish liturgical prayers of the time. Jesus probably intended that it would be used in public worship. If so, it is not only a prayer for individual disciples but as a group.

Both Jesus and the Talmudic writers emphasize God's watchful care. Rabbi Abahu observed: "The day of rain is greater than the resurrection of the dead, because the resurrection of the dead benefits only the just, but the rain benefits both the just and the unjust" (Tannit 7b).

The prayer initially accents not knowing the will of God but doing it: "Your will be done." It was assumed that God would make His way ever clearer as persons act on their current understanding.

Whereas the idea of hallowing (sanctifying) is difficult to get at, it was contrasted to profaning (desecration). Thus in rabbinic circles, the martyr was said to hallow God's name by maintaining his faith to the cruel end.

Three supplemental petitions follow: give us our daily bread, forgive us our trespasses, and lead us not into temptation. "When a person petitions God, he does not ask for wealth, but rather for his assigned or determined portion. This portion is what would be needed for sustenance--neither tremendous wealth nor poverty, but what is needed according to God's plan."[23] The sage does not ask for wealth that might be squandered, or poverty that robs him/her of the opportunity to do good.

Jesus exhorted His disciples also to forgive as they were forgiven.

> He understands the liberating power of forgiveness. A tremendous release occurs when one can forgive even the most heinous act. Jesus exemplifies forgiveness when he looks upon the Roman soldiers who are crucifying him. They are unaware of their offense and callous to the brutality of their actions[24]

He covets for His disciples what He would experience time and again in His life.

One can anticipate neither the strength of temptation or his/her ability to resist. So lead us not into temptation, but deliver us from the evil one. James comments: "Each one is tempted when, by his own evil desire, he is dragged away and enticed. Then, after desire has conceived, it gives birth to sin, and sin, when it is full grown, gives birth to death" (1:14-15).

Our attention focuses finally on fasting. It was an ancient and honored means of expressing one's humility and courting God's favor. David fasted in hope that God would spare the life of his son (2 Sam. 12:22). *Yom Kippur* (the Day of Atonement) prescribed fasting for all (Lev. 16:29). Jesus assumes the practice when it serves its intended purpose, and not engaged in for display.

Thus when John's disciples inquired of Jesus why His disciples were not fasting in their manner or that of the Pharisees, they likely had some specific or extended practice in mind (9:14). Whatever the situation, Jesus thought it inappropriate for the time being. His disciples will turn to fasting when He has taken His leave. He meant His disciples to fast when the circumstances called for it and not simply as a religious obligation.

Our social responsibilities are bound inexorably to our religious devotion (cf. 22:37-39). They grow out of our recognition that all were created in God's image and for His pleasure. There can be no exceptions, either within or without the household of faith.

"See that you do not look down on one of these little ones," Jesus warned (18:10). "For I tell you that their angels in heaven always see the face of the Father in heaven." That is, their ministering angels register their concern with God over those entrusted to their care.

The idea of guardian angels greatly expanded during the period following the Jewish exile. They filled a void created by the impression that God had distanced Himself.

While singling out children, Jesus quickly extended His range of concern to the *lost sheep* however applicable (18:12-14). This might include women, aliens, the poor, the aged, and the irreligious. It could be anyone society looked down upon, and incensed by its disregard. Zealous guardian angels ministered to them as well, and plead their cause before the Almighty.

Paul warned those eating food offered to idols that they might wound the conscience of some unnecessarily offended by the practice (1 Cor. 8:9-13). "So this weak brother, for whom Christ died, is destroyed for your knowledge." As if it were an offering on the altar of their vanity, and violating their responsibility for "these little ones."

The pillars of Jewish social ethics may be stated as reverence, solicitude, and freedom. There seems nothing in Jesus' admonitions that would lead us to imagine that He thought otherwise.

Reverence. Put simply, we ought not to use others as tools to serve our purposes. We should not manipulate others to achieve our end, but relate to them as persons.

This would exclude such matters as personal injury, exploitation, oppression, humiliation, or deprivation. He/she must be given ample time and opportunity to work through matters instead of surrendering to a forced solution. Once the decision has been made, we must allow it to stand. We also should permit persons to withhold thoughts they feel uncomfortable to express. In short, we must respect the God-given individuality of others.

As an example, Jesus admonished: "Do not judge, or you too will be judged" (7:1).

Judge (*krino*) often carries the connotation "condemn", and it is in that sense that it is used here. The use of our critical faculties in making value-judgments is frequently required in the New Testament, as in vv. 6 and 15-20 of the present chapter. There may be a place for verbal rebuke and even stronger measures (18:15-17). This passage, however, is concerned with the fault-finding, condemnatory attitude which is too often combined with a blindness to one's own faults (as lacking reverence for others).[25]

Solicitude. "I am sending you out like sheep among wolves," Jesus warned the disciples (10:16). "Therefore be as shrewd as snakes and as innocent as doves." Paul gave similar advice: "I want you to be wise about what is good, and innocent about what is evil" (Rom. 16:19).

Jesus told a story about a manager who was accused of wasting the resources entrusted to him (Luke 16:1f). Confronted with the prospect of losing his position, he accepted partial payment from his debtors, by that salvaging the situation. Jesus did not commend his behavior but observed his shrewdness. For "the people of this world" are more skillful in dealing with "their own kind," Jesus concluded, than are "the children of light."

The bottom line is this: social networking is a fragile enterprise. We must approach it with deliberate care, and concern for the others involved. We must take care to mend the relationships once they have become strained. We must look to God for grace to manage our social responsibilities well, and seek His forgiveness when we have wantonly gone astray.

Freedom. Few people, if any, have so prized freedom as the Hebrews. Denied liberty under the oppressive hand of Pharaoh, they came to revel in it for themselves and others. Rabbi Eckstein comments:

> In addition to recalling their exodus from Egypt long ago, Jews are also urged to actively pursue freedom for all those to whom it is presently denied. That is the meaning of the biblical command to love the stranger since you were once strangers in Egypt and can best understand their hearts.[26]

On the occasion of Jesus breaking bread with Matthew, the Pharisees questioned His disciples: "Why does your teacher eat with tax collectors and 'sinners'?" (9:11). They had built a fence that kept such people at arm's length. Jesus exercised His freedom to replace the fence with a bridge.

On another occasion, a Canaanite woman approached Jesus (15:22).

He had retired to the area to escape the pressures of ministry and controversy. (It appears to have been His strategy to build a strong Jewish power base before launching a mission to the Gentiles.)

"Lord, Son of David, have mercy on me!" she implored the Christ. In this and other ways, she kept on pleading with Jesus to exorcize her daughter. Jesus subsequently replied: "It is not right to take the children's bread and give it to the dogs." This is what she may have expected from a Jewish rabbi.

"Yes, Lord," she responded, "but even the dogs eat the crumbs that fall from their master's table." Recognizing Jesus' mission to Israel, she still held out for mercy. Jesus commended her faith, and granted her petition. It was her right to intercede, and His to respond within the limits set by His calling.

Freedom here and elsewhere must not be construed as license. Jesus exhorted persons to free themselves up to God and others, and so to fulfill their spiritual birthright. When we disregard others in pursuit of personal goals, we become enslaved to self.

We have weighed Jesus' concern for community concerning religious devotion and social involvement. It remains to touch on His ritual admonitions: "Take and eat" and "drink from it" (26:26-27). Marvin Wilson reconstructs the setting:

> It seems clear that Jesus instituted the Lord's Supper by associating it with the third cup of wine, which came after the Passover meal was eaten (cf, 1 Cor. 11:25). It was known as the "cup of redemption," which rabbinic tradition linked to the third of the fourfold promise of redemption in Exodus 6:6-7. He refused, however, to drink of the fourth cup (Mark 14:25; cf. 1 Cor. 11:25), referred to as the cup of consummation (cf. Exod. 6:7) based on the promise that God will take his own people to be with him.[27]

They were to take of the bread and wine in remembrance of Jesus' once-for-all sacrifice, and in anticipation of His return. In so doing, they would symbolize their oneness in Christ, in faith, and in hope. So often as they took of the common elements, it was a repudiation of apparent divisions within the body.

With such in mind, Paul encouraged those in Corinth to "wait for each other," so that they might partake together (1 Cor. 11:33). While they had once been strangers to God and one another, they were now the people of God for time and eternity.

Taking all into consideration, Jesus characteristically exhorted His disciples to live out what they had become, a caring community. One where none slips through the cracks between concern; one where we prize each as if a jewel of great worth.

Chapter 6

ITS MISSION

Jesus urged those who had *come* in faith to *go* in service. The world owed them nothing; they were committed to Christ for the world in everything.

How can we account for the early success of the church? No doubt there were many fortuitous circumstances: a base of operations among the Jewish people extended throughout the diaspora, the *Pax Romana* (Peace of Rome) providing relative security in travel, Hellenistic language and culture as a means of communication, a network of roads joining the far flung provinces of the Roman Empire, the collapse of traditional religious options, the need for a cosmopolitan faith to suit the time, the Godfearing Gentiles who shared the Jewish perspective without ethnic inhibitions, and so on. Even so, the ultimate answer lies elsewhere: with *Jesus* and the mandate to disciple all nations, with *Jesus* and the encouragement that all authority had been given to Him in heaven and earth, with *Jesus* and the promise that He would be with them always.

Magnificent Obsession

Jesus is Lord of all! (cf. Acts 10:26). So Peter concluded as the light began to penetrate the darkness of the pagan world around him. So are we repeatedly assured and in ingenious ways in Matthew's narrative.

Thomas Clarke acknowledges Jesus' lordship in three connections: in anticipatory fashion through His teaching and miracles, initially with His resurrection/ascension triumph, and eventually in "imaginative" response to the grace He extends.[28] Clarke elaborates: "He teaches and he heals. He is critical of his own social system, and he begins to form a community which will shape society in radically alternative ways. Inevitably his role as preacher, teacher, wonder-worker, community-builder, brings him into the role of suffering servant."

This anticipatory phase serves two purposes: it sets forth the paradox that success comes by way of service, and sets in place the paradigm of Jesus as exemplar. This is *not* the way the world views matters. It assumes that we succeed by exercising authority over others. "Not so with you," Jesus enjoined the disciples (20:26). "Instead, whoever wants to become great among you must be as your servant, and whoever wants to be first must be your slave."

Jesus provided the role model for the disciples. They observed His priorities, and rearranged theirs accordingly. They observed His sensitivity to the needs of others, and worked at being more sensitive. They observed His advocacy for the poor, and they embraced it heartily. As a result, they were called "Christians", as bearers of the image of Christ.

> The second phase of lordship which the reader will find here is the exercise of power by the risen Lord prior, in some fashion, to the response of Christians to his rule. ...The value of accenting it is primarily in rooting Christian hope not in our own fragile and fallible resources but in the power of God communicated to his victorious Son, our exalted Lord.

God wished it so, and we can not dissuade Him. God made it so, and nothing we can do will alter the results.

This recalls the counsel of Gamaliel. Having made mention that various Messianic pretenders came to naught, he concluded: "Let these men (the apostolic circle) alone! For if their purpose or activity is of human origin, it will fall. But if it is from God, you will not be able to stop these men, you will only find yourselves fighting against God" (Acts 38-39). Such was the confidence of the early disciples that they were engaged in God's work, and that which God set about to do would get done.

Finally, there is a sense in which Jesus' lordship becomes actual only as persons exercise the potential. It is *de jure* up to this point, and *de facto* after that.

We shift authors in the last connection. Joseph Weber observes: "The affirmation of Jesus Christ as Lord of one's personal life can be understood by most Christians. One's faith is lived out in one's daily, personal life. It makes a difference in how a person experiences and understands life."[29]

The experience of Zacchaeus provides a classic example. Welcoming Jesus to his home, the tax collector declared: "Look, Lord! Here and now I give half of my possessions to the poor, and if I have cheated anybody out of anything, I will pay back four times the amount" (Luke 19:8). Jesus was for him not simply Lord in word but in deed (cf. 6:46).

Weber deliberately presses on: "Christians also can usually understand that Jesus Christ is Lord of the Church. In the community of the Church this lordship is celebrated in worship and prayer, and responded to in obedience." Otherwise stated, the lordship of Christ is recalled in community, celebrated in community, and served through community.

Paul expressed his concern concerning divisions in the Corinthian Church (1 Cor. 10-12). One professed to follow Paul, another Apollos or Cephas, or even Christ--out of partisan purpose. This ought not to be, since there is only one Lord over all (8:6).

Weber raises a provocative question: "Christ exercises his lordship in the world through the church, but is he also to be affirmed as Lord in the world apart from the church?" Qualification aside, Paul speaks for the affirmative. "And God placed all things under his feet and appointed him to be head over everything for the church, which is his body, the fullness of him who fills everything in every way: (Eph. 1:22-23).

"All things" is inclusive, as is "everything" (repeated for emphasis). Concerning the "principalities and powers" which Christ subjects, these are variously interpreted: as demonic forces, oppressive political structures, and dehumanizing social networks. All may be implied.

Jesus exercises His authority over the world as to benefit the church. All things may be said to work together for good not only for individuals who believe (Rom. 8:28), but for the community as a whole. If, as intended, it learns from its failures as well as successes.

Weber finishes on a triumphant note:

> The eschatological hope in which the Church lives because of Christ's victory over the principalities and powers is a hope for all the world. The Church as the new creation is the sign that the new creation is intended for all the world. ...Both (Church and world) live in the light of his victory over the principalities and powers.[30]

This calls for Christians to assume their responsibility for the task set before them. They need to strain to hear Jesus' speak above the clamor of society, and move out in faith to do His bidding. There is no alternative but to admit failure.

This Do

Pleased to hear Jesus invite them to come, some resist His exhortation to go. They would bask in the warmth of those of like perspective and interests. They prefer not to encounter those who disagree or may prove hostile.

Jesus does not allow that option. "You are the light of the world" (5:14), He insisted. A city located on a hill can not be hidden. Persons do not put a lamp under a bowl but on a stand, so that it will provide light for all. "In the same way, let your light shine before men, that they may see your good deeds and praise your Father in heaven."

Ulrich Luz describes *light* as "an open metaphor," seeing it can be variously applied: to righteous persons, the Torah, Israel, the Servant of the Lord, or Jerusalem.[31] Here the reference is to Jesus' disciples. They are not to hide away in a cloister, but go into the world as *light* and *salt*.

The obligation to go no doubt embraces more than geographical considerations. The disciple must be prepared to meet others where they are and in terms of their perceived needs. He/she must be willing to work from the known to the unknown, and so encourage a pilgrimage of faith. He/she must be prepared to go the second mile when called upon only to go one.

As you go, preach (10:7)! Preach that the long-awaited kingdom of God is breaking into history. Alert persons to that this is the day of salvation.

We ought to keep the message simple. Jesus has died for our sins, and raised for our justification. Those who repent of their sins, and put their faith in the risen Lord have passed from death to life. The future holds nothing for them to fear.

Preach with urgency. Once we reject Jesus' gracious offer, it becomes increasingly hard to respond. Time is not in our favor: the day is far spent and the night at hand.

Preach confidently. The word will bear bountiful fruit if received into good soil (13:23). It will, in any case, accomplish what God purposes (Isa. 55:11).

As you go, heal (10:8). This imperative ties in with the preceding one:

> The message about the coming of God's rule must be rendered believable through concrete demonstrations of God's caring. The modern church understands this principle and tries to be faithful to it. Mission boards send out not only evangelists but medical personnel, educators, agricultural missionaries, and others who will communicate the living

gospel through visible acts of compassion.³²

Jesus accents compassionate concern above supernatural authentication. *God* heals in Jewish tradition, despite the means He may select. The rabbis urged that we not put God to the test by demanding that it be by way of miracle (cf. 4:7). Whatever results, the righteous trust their way to God.

Concerning miracles, C.S. Lewis reminds us that they do not occur in any uniform fashion even in Holy Writ. They focus for the most part around revelatory events, such as the exodus, the contest of the Hebrew prophets with Baal, the advent of Jesus, and the acts of the apostles.

As you go, let down and draw in your nets (fish). It is not enough to speak out, but we must draw our net in (5:19; cf. 13:47). The accent seems to be on persuasion.

Agrippa contemptuously responded to the appeal of Paul: "Do you think that in such a short time you can persuade me to be a Christian?" (Acts 26:28). The apostle stoutly replied: "Short time or long--I pray God that not only you but all who are listening to me today may become what I am, except for these chains." Such was his commitment to persuading persons of their need of Christ and salvation in Him.

As you go, disciple. "Therefore go and make disciples of all nations, baptizing them...and teaching them to obey everything I have commanded you" (28:19-20). Disciple all irrespective of ethnic derivation. Disciple to Christ in contrast to self. Disciple thoroughly with no matter left unattended.

> Matthew apparently can take for granted that the missionaries will proclaim the good news and call for faith (see 24:1-4; 18:6); what he cannot take for granted is that the converts will treat seriously Jesus' moral demands. He is deeply distressed by the number of so-called converts who think they can attend the Messiah's wedding feast in the shabby rags of their old pagan morality (see 22:11-14).³³

The tendency to which the text refers was in Jesus' time already all too evident and exceedingly disconcerting.

That this problem continued to plague the church, and tarnish its witness can be seen in Paul's caustic reaction: "It is actually reported that there is sexual immorality among you, and of a kind that does not occur even among pagans" (1 Cor. 5:1). They had not fulfilled their obligation to disciple.

As you go, do good deeds (cf. 5:16). The centrality of *mitzvot* (good deeds, albeit this does not do justice to the original) to Jewish piety can hardly be overstated.

> The mitzvot sanctify the Jew's life and imbue it with transcendent meaning and content. Daily the Jew prays, "For they (the mitzvot) are our lives and the length of our days and upon these we will meditate day and night." The mitzvot are the vehicles by which Israel is transformed into a kingdom of priests and a holy nation; they are the divinely ordained tools enabling her to emulate God's ways.[34]

Through *mitzvot*, persons cooperated with God in His benevolent concern for the universe. Through *mitzvot*, they would partake of the divine mystery. Through *mitzvot*, they would help restore what went wrong.

James consequently concluded: "Show me your faith without deeds, and I will show you my faith by what I do. You believe that there is one God. Good! Even the demons believe that--and shudder" (2:18-19). Jesus enjoined His disciples to couple word with deed in ministering to their generation.

As you go, pray that God will conscript others for the missionary task force. Jesus paused in His demanding ministry to observe: "The harvest is plentiful but the workers are few" (9:37). Petition "the Lord of the harvest" to send forth laborers to get in the crop.

Scripture often speaks of impending judgment as if the time of harvest (Isa. 37:12; Joel 3:13). It was in this context that John the Baptist warned: "His winnowing fork is in his hand, and he will clear his threshing floor, gathering his wheat into the barn and burning up the chaff with unquenchable fire" (3:12). Jesus similarly picked up on the theme: "The harvest is the end of the age, and the harvesters are angels" (13:39).

Here the harvesters are not the angels, as might be expected, but missionaries sent to rescue persons from perdition. If rejected, the opportunity will be lost.

The need is as pressing today as in Jesus' time. While the numbers of workers have increased, so has the opportunity. The field has expanded far beyond the modest soil of Israel. There are encouraging reports from many regions. There are also the urgent pleas for help that disturb our complacency.

We require no new strategy; we go with the one in hand. Pray that God will move upon hearts to serve Him gladly. Be open to His leading in our lives. Leave no stone unturned.

Go without anxiety. "*I* (emphatic) am sending you out like sheep among wolves" (10:16). As Bonhoeffer was want to say: grace is *costly* because it calls us to follow, but *grace* because we follow Christ. The prospect of living among ferocious protagonists would be enough to intimidate the most courageous person, but with Christ we can face the worst of situations.

Like Master, like servant. "If it is possible, may this cup be taken from me. Yet not as I will, but as you will" (26:39). No healthy person welcomes adversity or persecution. No wise person shuns it if within God's providential purpose.

Suffer, if need be, for doing good and not for evil (cf. 1 Pet. 1:13-17). Be "innocent as doves." The wisdom and innocence of the disciples sharply contrasts with the wickedness of the oppressors.

Guard yourselves against the wolves that prowl seeking who they may devour. Obviously, do not invite trouble. Do not even take unnecessary chances.

When they manage to drag you before the magistrate, do not worry what you shall say. "And that time you will be given what to say, for it will not be you speaking, but the Spirit of the Father speaking through you" (10:19). God will provide what you require. Trust in Him.

Go rejoicing. "Blessed are the poor in spirit, for theirs is the kingdom of heaven" (5:3). Blessed also are those who mourn, hunger and thirst for righteousness, the merciful, pure in heart, peacemakers, and persecuted. They shall be comforted, inherit the earth, filled, shown mercy, see God, designated the sons of God, and possess the kingdom of heaven. "Blessed are you when people insult you, persecute you and falsely say all kinds of evil against you because of me. Rejoice and be glad, because great is your reward in heaven, for in the same way, they persecuted the prophets who were before you."

Jesus' appraisal of what constitutes a genuinely blessed life appears diametrically opposed to what passes as conventional wisdom. The world thinks that happiness consists in wealth, power, and indulgence. Jesus' life and ministry accents devotion and service.

Where does such happiness come from? From within. From out of a heart filled to overflowing with God's love. In addition, cultivated in a fellowship of those who have responded to Jesus' invitation to come, and take seriously His challenge to go.

Chapter 7

THE CONSUMMATION

"As it was in the days of Noah, so it will be at the coming of the Son of Man," Jesus confided (24:37). "Those alive *in the days of Noah* are not pictured as especially wicked. Absorbed in the daily round of living, they were taken unawares by the flood."[35] They lived for the tempting present instead of preparing for the inevitable future.

Conversely, Jesus' disciples were not so much driven by the past as drawn by the future. He urged them to plan well and keep on course. While there is much in the world to distract us, press on. While there are those who would dissuade us, press on. While discouraged by events, keep pressing on. There is a light at the end of the tunnel.

The Blessed Hope

Matthew records as the order of anticipated events: the Lord's return, judgment, and eternal consequences. Signs will precede this climax to redemptive history.

As Jesus was walking away from the temple, the disciples called His attention to its lavish construction. "Do you see all these things?" Jesus inquired (24:2). "I tell you a truth, not one stone here will be left on another; every one will be thrown down."

Jesus' announcement of the destruction of the temple likely came as a surprise to the disciples. They waited until He was alone with them, overlooking the temple area from the Mount of Olives, to ask: "When will this happen, and what will be the sign of your coming and of the end of the age?" A single definite article in the latter instance suggests that Jesus' disciples expected His coming and the close of the age to coincide.

Jesus tailored His response to distinguish between the two. While Jerusalem's days were numbered, His return remained indefinite, following a time of severe tribulation. False prophets would abound and deceive many. The gospel would be preached as a testimony to all nations. There would be a desecration resembling the pagan altar raised by Antiochus Epiphanes in the temple precinct. There would be cosmic disturbances. "At which time the sign of the Son of Man will appear in the sky" (24:30), as did the star at His birth.

"They will see the Son of man coming on the clouds of the sky, with power and great glory." At which, the nations will mourn. For they will realize how wrong they have been in rejecting His offer of clemency.

The trumpet's sound will bid the elect to gather from the four winds, from one end of the heavens to the other. The Son of Man's coming will be audible as well of visible. There will be no mistaking His return, nor hope of frustrating His purpose in returning.

"When the Son of Man comes in his glory, and all the angels with him, he will sit on his throne in heavenly glory. All the nations will come to him, and he will separate the people one from another as a shepherd separates the sheep from the goats" (25:31-32). This will be based on how they have treated "the least of these brothers of mine," as if in response to Jesus Himself.

"These brothers of mine" is variously interpreted: as those in need, the Jewish remnant, Christians in general, or those engaged in missionary activity. The last of these options seems most in keeping with the context. As one reacts to the one sent, so he responds to the One sending.

Even so, we may err in stressing one option to the exclusion of others. This may illustrate what we sometimes designate a *fuzzy set*, not meant to be too precise. Instead of either/or, it could be understood as both/and.

Certain of Jesus' references to reward seem best understood in relation to the final judgment. As for those persecuted and falsely accused, they will receive an ample reward (5:12). As for those who love their enemies, their reward also will be great (5:44,46). The Father who sees in secret will reward openly (6:4).

So also Jesus warned of retribution. "Anyone who is angry with his brother will be subject to judgment" (5:21). "For in the same way you judge others, you will be judged, and with the measure you use, it will be measured to you" (7:2). "You snakes! You brood of vipers! How will you escape being condemned to hell?" (23:33).

C.S. Lewis wrote convincingly of heaven and hell as "the great divorce," in the work by that title. He implied that a seemingly minor shift in direction, given time, would result in far different destinations. In the *Problem of Pain*, he concluded God knows (as we do not) when nothing more will serve to change our minds. There will be no turning back.

"We are at once struck with the remarkable reserve on the subject of heaven in the synoptics. No details are given about the contents of heaven. There are no flights of imagination."[36] On the other hand, many references underline its great importance.

Heaven is where God dwells. All else dims by comparison. As we recall, Jesus taught His disciples to address God as "our Father in heaven" (6:9).

Heaven is associated with doing God's will: "Your will be done on earth *as it is in heaven*" (6:10). Here those who delight to do God's will, shall have their desire realized. There will be no restraints put on their efforts. They will be encouraged at every juncture.

Heaven also is associated with angels (cf. 24:36), but only in passing. More characteristic of Matthew's narrative, they appear as messengers, guardians, and celestial warriors--the last concerning the coming of the Son of Man in glory.

Heaven opens its gates to the righteous. "Come, you who are blessed by my Father, take your inheritance, the kingdom prepared for you since the creation of the world" (25:34). "For I was hungry and you gave me something to eat, I was thirsty and you gave me something to drink, I was a stranger and you invited me in, I was sick and you looked after me, I was in prison and you came to visit me" (25:35-36).

The *righteous* respond: "Lord, when did we see you hungry and feed you, or thirsty and give you something to drink? When did we see you a stranger and invite you in, or needing clothes and clothe you? When did we see you sick or in prison and go to visit you?" Then the King will reply: "I tell you the truth, whatever you did for one of the least of these brothers of mine, you did for me."

The text deals in more specific terms with hell than heaven, and with approximate emphasis. The term *Gehenna* is employed seven times (5:22,29,30; 10:28; 18:19; 23:15,23). *Hades* occasionally is used in a comparable sense for eternal punishment (11:23; 16:18).

Gehenna, referring to the Valley of Hinnom, was notorious because of the idolatrous practices carried out there in the days of Ahaz and Manasseh. We read of the latter: "He sacrificed his own son in the fire, practiced sorcery and divination, and consulted mediums and spiritists" (2 Kings 21:6).

By Jesus' time, the valley served to accommodate the disposal of trash, providing a smoldering flame and giving off putrid odor. Hell was void of hope. That cast aside was no longer of use.

Scripture represents hell as pitch blackness, where there will be "weeping and gnashing of teeth" (8:12, cf. 13:42,50; 22:13; 24:51; 25:30). Initially, the contrast was between that of the brightly lit banquet hall and the darkness without.

The phrase "weeping and gnashing of teeth" seemingly combine the ideas of pain and anger, perhaps as if to suggest utter frustration. Thinking that they had no need of God, those who inhabit hell find this the bitterest of alternatives. If, as Lewis insists, hell remains the only place a loving God provides for those who will receive nothing better, there is little consolation for those so disposed. Life goes on, but we cannot imagine that things could get much worse.

Living Toward the Future

The most striking set of exhortations concerning the future focuses on Christ. They remind us that "this *same* Jesus, who has been taken from you into heaven, will come back in the same way you have seen him go into heaven" (Acts 1:11). They insist that "the Lord *himself* will come down from heaven" (1 Thess. 4:16). "In the future you will see the Son of Man sitting at the right hand of the Mighty One and coming in the clouds of heaven" (25:64).

Jesus began to denounce those towns in which many of His miracles took place, because they failed to repent. "Woe, to you Korazin! Woe to you, Bethsaida! If the miracles performed in you had been performed in Tyre and Sidon, they would have repented long ago in sackcloth and ashes. But I tell you, it will be more bearable for Tyre and Sidon on the day of judgment than for you" (11:21-22).

Tyre and Sidon had come to represent pagan disregard for the counsel of God (cf. Isa. 23; Ezek. 26-28). Their offense, though grave, shrank in comparison with these Galilean villages--according to the principle that to whom much is given, more shall be required. One greater than the prophets had visited them, with mightier deeds but little by way of response.

On another occasion, Jesus exhorted the disciples: "Watch out that no one deceive you" (24:4). For many will come claiming to be the Christ, and deceiving many. There will be wars and rumors of wars, but this is not the end. There will be persecution and martyrdom, but this is not the end. The gospel will be preached throughout the whole earth, "and then the end will come."

Beware and be faithful to declaring the gospel. The end will come in due time. Work while it is yet day, for the night is at hand.

"Now learn this lesson from the fig tree: As soon as its twigs get tender and its leaves come out, you know that summer is near. Even so, when you see all these things, you know that it is near, right at the door" (24:32-33). This generation will not pass away until all these things have happened. It seems unlikely that Jesus meant to say that He would return within the life time of those standing there. As noted earlier, He deliberately contrasts *these things* in connection to the destruction of Jerusalem with *that day* when He would return and bring matters to a successful conclusion. He expressly states that no one knows the latter time, none but His Father in heaven.

"Therefore keep watch," Jesus enjoined those about Him (24:42). Be expectant so not to put off necessary concerns, not squander precious time on trivial matters. Be prepared so enthusiastically to greet the return of Christ. Be on guard so not to be taken in by false prophets. However else it may apply, be certain to keep watch.

To illustrate His point and seemingly confirm our understanding, Jesus told a parable concerning ten virgins (25:1-13). Five were foolish and took no oil with them for their lamps. Five were wise and prepared for any eventuality. Seeing "the bridegroom was *a long time* in coming," they fell asleep. When at last roused from their sleep with the news of his arrival, the foolish maidens had exhausted their oil. When they had replenished their supply, it was too late. Jesus repeats His admonition for emphasis: "Keep watch, because you do not know the day or the hour."

Jesus introduces Himself as the judge at "that day" (7:21), in the role commonly attributed to God. The claim is the more striking for being assumed rather than argued.

> Whereas Mark emphasizes the necessity of accepting Jesus as the crucified Christ and following him on the path of self-denial, Matthew's stress is on manifesting one's devotion to Jesus as Lord by obeying his ethical instructions. The righteousness that surpasses that of the scribes and Pharisees (5:20) consists not in possessing the teachings of Jesus but in acting upon them.[37]

Those who obey might be said to believe. Without obedience, our rationalizations count for nothing.

A second set of exhortations deals with rewards and retribution. "Do not store up for yourselves treasures on earth, where moth and rust destroy, and where thieves break in and steal. But store up for yourselves treasures in heaven, where moth and rust do not destroy, and where thieves do not break in and steal" (6:19-20). Where your treasure is, there will be your heart as well.

> These verses challenge the equation of a person's worth with his or her acquisitions. Treasured clothing (a woman's dowry often consisted, in part, of expensive textiles) is vulnerable to insects. Wooden chests and books are subject to destruction by worms. Treasures that cannot be eaten can be stolen.[38]

The list could readily be extended. "Jesus' followers are instructed to avoid such insecurity by accumulating an invulnerable treasure consisting of kindnesses performed for the glory of God."

Some time later, Jesus told a parable concerning talents (25:14-30). A certain man was going on a journey, and entrusted his property to servants: to one five talents, another two, and still another one--each according to his ability. Upon returning, he demanded an accounting.

He who had received five, returned ten; he who had received two, returned four; but he who received one, had only one to show for his stewardship. The former received their master's commendation: "Well done, good and faithful servant! You have been faithful with a few things; I will put you in charge of many things. Come and share your master's happiness." As for the servant given one talent, the master rebukes him for being wicked and lazy. "Take the talent from him and give it to the one who has the ten talents. And throw that worthless servant outside, into the darkness, where there will be weeping and gnashing of teeth."

We are to suppose that each person is a steward of the gifts he or she is given. No two are the same. Each will be held accountable, not for the gifts of others but his/her own.

Reward and retribution in this context implies a greater opportunity of service on the one hand, or a loss of opportunity on the other. Use it or lose it.

On two occasions, Jesus asserts it better to mutilate oneself than perish (5:29-30; 18:8-9). While some have thought this a reference to excommunication, it more likely refers to renouncing such things as may tempt us. Step back from the precipice!

A third set of exhortations relates to usurping God's prerogative in judging. "Do not judge, or you too will be judged" (7:1). In the way we judge, we shall be judged.

As noted earlier, the accent here is on condemning. There are times when critical appraisal proves necessary, and rebuke perhaps called for. However, we must bear in mind that our perception is not only superficial but biased. "How do you look at the speck of sawdust in your brother's eye and pay no attention to the plank in your own eye?" Jesus pointedly inquired.

He subsequently told a parable concerning an enemy who secretively sowed weeds among the wheat, and went away (13:24-30). Now, when the weeds began to grow, the servants asked whether they should be removed. "No," the owner answered, "because while you are pulling the weeds, you may root up the wheat with them." Let the two grow together, and they will be separated at harvest time.

The appearance of *some* weeds would not have surprised the servants. It was their quantity that spurred them to action. They felt threatened by the number and persuasiveness of the false teachers among them. Jesus nonetheless, and likely for that reason, counseled restraint. Those who allow themselves to be governed by circumstances are not genuinely free to act on Jesus' admonitions.

The theme resonates in another context. Jesus had vigorously attacked the Pharisees for setting aside the word of God for the traditions of men (15:6). The disciples were concerned, and questioned Jesus: "Do you know that the Pharisees were offended when they heard this?" Jesus responded to them: "Every plant that my heavenly Father has not planted will be pulled up by the roots. Leave them; they are blind guides. If a blind man leads a blind man, both will fall into a pit."

While one can err by rejecting what God accepts, the reverse also can be true. We can go astray by embracing what God rejects. Let them alone, lest you perish with them.

It is not the severity of God's judgment that comes across in such instances, but His unmitigated fairness. No one can hope to confound or resist Him. As Karl Barth was want to say: "Let God be God!"

The future may be said to start *now!* Thus when Peter and Andrew heard Jesus' invitation to follow, they left all and followed. Thus when Jesus announced to the centurion to return home to his restored servant, he obediently went. Thus when Jesus instructed the disciples to feed the multitude, they presented their meager resources.

Conversely, the would-be disciple requested that he first be allowed to fulfill his family obligation. The religious elite chose to quibble over the finer points of the Torah than repent. Some conspired to put Jesus to death as if to postpone the inevitable.

Whatever the future holds, we can know Who holds the future. Those who trust their ways to Christ are in the best of hands. Those who reject him experience inevitable loss. Jesus speaks, as if a voice out of the past, calling us to take inventory of our lives. Jesus speaks, as if in the present, urging us to put our house in order.

EPILOGUE

We come to summarize our findings. First, we discovered no set of abstract principles, as if unrelated to the gospel narrative. Jesus exhorted His disciples concerning His Messianic leverage. They responded because of their devotion to Him. Remove Jesus from the mix, and the ethical imperatives come tumbling down as would a house of cards.

Otherwise put, Jesus exhorted as a teacher does his students. His admonitions were directives for disciples. If others were to see wisdom in Jesus' teaching, well and good. This resembles a byproduct.

Jesus calls persons to live by a standard distinct from that of the world. They must live according to surpassing righteousness, exhibited by unconditional love. Beyond outer conformity, it concerns itself with inner rectitude. Rather than simply taking Jesus as an example, it cultivates a dynamic relationship.

As Luz correctly observes: "Jesus' ethics is one of contrast, formulated on the basis of the coming of the kingdom of God, which is different from the world. To love on the basis of this ethics means to display to the world a sign of the 'wholly other'--kingdom of God."[39] We are more impressed by its discontinuity than conventionality.

Even so, Jesus drew from prophetic tradition to discuss surpassing righteousness. He expressly denied coming to destroy the Torah, but instead to fulfill it. He repeatedly pressed the discussion back to the original intent of God in giving the particular instruction.

Jesus' ethic was a refinement and extension of Torah. God does not say one thing yesterday and another today. Quite the reverse! He progressively reveals His truth, building on what has gone before, teaching the unknown by way of the known. He proceeds much as parents set out to instruct those entrusted to their care.

Jesus' ethic calls upon the world to reexamine itself. As Emil Brunner would say: "No culture is so perfect that the gospel will not critique it." Culture reveals the imperfection of those who fashion it: with advantage for the rich and disadvantage to the poor, with advantage for the power brokers and disadvantage to the powerless, with advantage for those with connections and disadvantage to those lacking them. Culture needs to hear now and again the prophetic voice: "But let justice roll on like a river, righteousness like a never-failing stream!" (Amos 5:24).

Do not confuse conventional wisdom with the kingdom of God. Our crusades, legitimate as they may be, fall pitifully short. Nothing less than the unqualified will of God will suffice in Jesus' perspective.

Jesus' ethic involves life together. Each came by way of Christ to community. These became the people of God by virtue of the blood of Christ. They were bonded together for time and eternity.

Friedrick Gogarten described this community as being responsible for one another, and open to God's creative leading. Just so! Each was to be there for others, and allow others to be there for him/her. They were individually and corporately to be not simply willing but anxious to for God's guidance.

This would involve coming and going. They would come apart to recognize their uniqueness and unity. They would go in demanding service. The rhythm of coming and going would persist from beginning to end. It would mark their character as a Messianic community.

Jesus' ethic was cultivated by hope. What He had begun, He would bring to a successful conclusion. Those who cooperate, do so with confidence. Those who resist, find that their time is running short.

So it was with the martyr. It was not that he/she lacked an appreciation for life and could surrender it easily. Quite the reverse! The martyr cherished life so deeply that he/she would rather have the days cut short and enjoy life for eternity.

We must steer clear of two opposite pitfalls: the tendency to withdraw from the world on the one hand, and conform on the other. Either we draw back out of a false sense of piety, or allow the world to set our agenda. As Karl Barth in his *Humanity of God* described the latter: "We leave the door and windows open for the (cultural) winds to blow."

It seems obvious that Jesus intended the disciples to live in creative tension with the world. They were caught as if between heaven and earth. Their heads being in the clouds, their feet must remain firmly on the ground. In this regard, they were true heirs of the lamenting prophets.

As if to summarize, Jesus exhorted those who would be His disciples to "take my yoke upon you and learn of me, for I am gentle and humble in heart, and you will find rest for your souls" (11:29). *His* yoke proves to be easy and *His* burden light.

The yoke of Christ contrasts to the heavy load imposed by His contemporaries (23:4). "Although the requirements of the kingdom are great (5:17-20), they appear in a different light when seen as expressions of loving obedience rather than demands for religious achievement."[40] Love does not reckon the cost.

ENDNOTES

1. Richard Hires, *Jesus and Ethics*, pp. 11-17.
2. Ibid., p. 126.
3. Samuel Sandmel, *A Jewish Understanding of the New Testament*, p. 29.
4. R.T. France, *Matthew*, p. 193.
5. C.G. Montefiore, "Jesus and the Rabbis," *Jesus* (Anderson, ed.), p. 156.
6. France, *op. cit.*, p. 160.
7. J. Ramsey Michaels, "The Kingdom of God and the Historical Jesus," *The Kingdom of God in 20th-Century Interpretation* (Willis, ed.), p. 111.
8. George Ladd, *A Theology of the New Testament*, p. 62.
9. France, *op. cit.*, p. 209.
10. Ladd, *op. cit.*, p. 342.
11. B.T. Viviano, "The Kingdom of God in the Qumran Literature," *The Kingdom of God in 20th-Century Interpretation* (Willis, ed.), p. 107.
12. Leonhard Goppelt, *Theology of the New Testament*, Vol. 1, p. 118.
13. Donald Hagner, *Matthew 14-28*, p. 517.
14. Donald Guthrie, *New Testament Theology*, p. 331.
15. W.F. Albright and C.S. Mann, *Matthew*, p. 58.
16. Ibid., p. 231.
17. Ulrich Luz, *Matthew 1-7*, p. 270.
18. Robert Mounce, *Matthew*, p. 160.
19. France, *op. cit.*, p. 256.
20. Guthrie, *op. cit.*, p. 709.
21. Robert Gundry, *Matthew*, p. 102.
22. Mounce, *op. cit.*, pp. 54-55.
23. Brad Young, *The Jewish Background to the Lord's Prayer*, p. 24.
24. Ibid., p. 30.
25. France, *op. cit.*, p. 142.

26. Yechiel Eckstein, *What Christians Should Know About Jesus and Judaism*, p. 104.
27. Marvin Wilson, *Our Father Abraham*, pp. 246-247.
28. Thomas Clarke (ed.), *Above Every Name*, pp. 3-4.
29. Joseph Weber, "Christ's Victory over the Powers," *Above Every Name* (Clarke, ed.), p. 66.
30. Ibid., p. 80.
31. Luz, *op cit.*, pp. 251-252.
32. Douglas Hare, *Matthew*, p. 111.
33. Ibid., p. 333.
34. Eckstein, *op. cit.*, p. 69.
35. Mounce, *op. cit.*, p. 229.
36. Guthrie, *op. cit.*, p. 875.
37. Hare, *op. cit.*, p. 82.
38. Ibid., p. 71.
39. Luz, *op. cit.*, p. 459.
40. Mounce, *op. cit.*, p. 104.

BIBLIOGRAPHY

Albright, W.F. and C.S. Mann. *Matthew*. New York: Doubleday, 1971.
Anderson, Hugh. *Jesus*. Englewood Cliffs: Prentice-Hall, 1967.
Clarke, Thomas (ed.). *Above Every Name*. Ramsey: Paulist, 1980.
Eckstein, Yechiel. *What Christians Should Know About Jews and Judaism*. Waco: Word, 1984.
France, R.T. *Matthew*. Grand Rapids: Eerdmans, 1985.
Goppelt, Leonhard. *Theology of the New Testament*, Vol. 1. Grand Rapids: Eerdmans, 1986.
Gundry, Robert. *Matthew*. Grand Rapids: Eerdmans, 1994.
Guthrie, Donald. *New Testament Theology*. Downers Grove: Inter-Varsity, 1981.
Hagner, Donald. *Matthew 14-28*. Dallas: Word, 1995.
Hare, Douglas. *Matthew*. Louisville: John Knox, 1993.
Hires, Richard. *Jesus and Ethics*. Philadelphia: Westminster, 1968.
Ladd, George. *A Theology of the New Testament*. Grand Rapids: Eerdmans, 1974.
Luz, Ulrich. *Matthew 1-7*. Minneapolis: Augsburg, 1989.
Michaels, J. Ramsay. "The Kingdom of God and the Historical Jesus," The Kingdom of God in 20th-Century Interpretation (Willis, ed.), 109-118.
Montefiore, C.G. "Jesus and the Rabbis," *Jesus* (Anderson, ed.), 156-157.
Mounce, Robert. *Matthew*. Peabody: Hendrickson, 1991.
Sandmel, Samuel. *A Jewish Understanding of the New Testament*. New York: KTAV, 1956.
Viviano, B.T. "The Kingdom of God in the Qumran Literature," *The Kingdom of God in 20th-Century Interpretation* (Willis, ed.), 97-107.
Weber. Joseph. "Christ's Victory over the Powers," *Above Every Name* (Clarke, ed.), 66-82.
Willis, Wendell (ed.). *The Kingdom of God in 20th-Century Interpretation*. Peabody: Hendricksen, 1987.
Wilson, Marvin. *Our Father Abraham*. Grand Rapids: Eerdmans, 1989.

Young, Brad. *The Jewish Background to the Lord's Prayer*. Austin: Center for Judaic-Christian Studies, 1984.

INDEX

"come, follow me," 1, 4, 11-12, 14-15
Communion, 41-42
community, 33-42
consummation, 5, 51-58
disciple(s): 1-3, 5, 10-11, 13, 15, 19, 27, 33, 37-38, 40, 44, 46-47, 51, 60-61
ekklesia (assembly, church), 19, 34-35
   see community
ethics, 6-7, 59
    ethics and eschatology, 6
    ethics as eschatology, 6
    ethics as realized eschatology, 7
    ethics without eschatology, 6
faith/belief, 14, 21, 23, 43, 55
fasting, 38-39
freedom, 40-41
Gehenna (Valley of Hinnom, hell), 37, 52-54
giving, 5, 36
   see *mitzvot,* 48
gospel, 4, 55
heaven, 52, 53
"I say to you," 29-31
"it is written," 27-28
Jesus, 2
    as a Galilean, 2
    as Lord, 43-45
    as concerns personal redemption, 12-13
    as to physical characteristics, 2
    as to public ministry, 2
    as to redemptive history, 13-14
    as to the redemption of creation, 14

kingdom of heaven (God), 1, 4, 17-23, 46, 59
krino (judge), 39-40, 56-57
love, 29, 31, 59
Messiah (Christ, anointed), 4, 10-16, 55
Messianic ambiguity, 10-11
mission, 5, 43-49
mitzvot (good deeds), 31, 48
multitude, 2-3, 11, 57
obedience, 3, 14, 31, 55, 57
paraklesis (exhortation), ix, 4
plerosai (fulfill), 26
Pharisees, 13, 19-20, 23, 26, 30-31, 57
prayer, 37-38, 45
rejoicing, 49
repentance, 1, 14, 17, 20, 23, 54
reverence, 39-40
rewards and retribution, 5, 52-56
righteousness, 13, 22, 31, 36, 59
the Scriptures, 25-31
solicitude, 40
Torah (teaching, law), 18, 25, 26-27, 29, 31

Part II

UP FROM THE DEPTHS
(Mark As Tragedy)

PREFACE

"Comedy aims at representing men as worse," according to Aristotle, "tragedy as better than in actual life."[1] Comedy exposes their folly; tragedy their potential in the face of seemingly overwhelming obstacles.

Mark's Gospel accents the tragic dimension of life. Gilbert Bilezikian accordingly reflects: "His future Gospel was in search of an appropriate mold. It is therefore not inconceivable that, faced with a challenge calling for literary skills beyond his own, Mark was attracted to the dominant literary model of his day."[2]

Moreover, "For Mark the supreme act of Christian liberation may well have been to proclaim the universal relevance of a very Jewish story by telling it in the manner of a Greek tragedy."[3] In any case, he succeeded in emphasizing the universal relevance of the gospel.

Whether he was even conscious of his reliance on the tragic genre is open to question. It was, as Bilezikian reminds us, "the dominant literary model of his day." Mark was sensitive to his cultural heritage and media of communication.

I intend to take a fresh look at Mark's Gospel through the prism of tragedy. This suggests for its major divisions the complication (1:1-8:21), crisis (8:22-9:1), and denouement (11:1-16:8). We will touch on each of these in turn.

Up From the Depths also calls attention to the tragic perspective on life. "Out of the depths I cry to you, O Lord, hear my voice. Let your ears be attentive to my cry for mercy" (Psa. 130:1). The psalmist's faith transformed "out of" to "up from" the depths of despair.

This endeavor may recall an earlier work, *Celebrating Jesus as Lord*. The former explored Matthew's Gospel concerning its likely construction as a lectionary, strikingly pertinent for subsequent times. Both strive to appreciate literary style as a clue to better understanding Biblical content.

Even so, they reveal contrasting approaches. Matthew invites us to celebrate all that God has done, is doing, and will do by way of His Anointed. Mark encourages us courageously to confront failure, suffering, and death in fellowship with Christ. Each serves in its distinctive fashion to minister to would-be disciples. God makes no mistakes.

These are critical times in which to live. We have developed weapons that can destroy life as we know it. The fabric of society appears threatened by moral decay. Heroism seems diminished with the passing of time. Mark's Gospel thus appears very timely, as if hand in glove.

Chapter 1

TRAGIC HERO

Complication chronicles the rising action, *denouement* the falling action, and *crisis* the turning point between the two. The *complication* concludes with Jesus' question: "Do you still not understand?" (8:21). The healing of the blind man at Bethsaida anticipates the disciples' dawning realization of Jesus' Messianic character. *Now*, at long last, they understood.

Mark's opening sentence introduces us to the tragic hero. "The pattern of complication receives full development early in the Gospel as Jesus begins to move, work, and teach among people left mystified by His obvious uniqueness and yet unable to draw appropriate conclusions."[4]

Jesus, God's Anointed

"The beginning of the gospel about Jesus Christ, the Son of God" (1:1), Mark enthusiastically reports.

> Although "Christ" does not have the definite article before it here, nevertheless it does not yet seem to have become merely a personal name or surname (which it virtually becomes in the Epistles). It is therefore still a title, and so, even without the article, equivalent to the Hebrew "Messiah", "God's Anointed", whether or not Mark's Gentile readers understood the full meaning of the word.[5]

What they may have lacked in understanding could help them identify with those who struggled to penetrate the awesome mystery that Jesus projected.

We read that "the people were amazed at His teaching, because He taught as one who had authority, not as the teachers of the law" (1:22). (The latter relied on precedent, much as with our legal code today.) They were "completely amazed" when Jesus came walking on the water (6:51). One surprise did not prepare them adequately for the next.

"Inasmuch as the reader knows from the very beginning that Jesus is the Christ, the Son of God, there is never any question of a Messianic Secret *for the reader of the gospel*."[6] The reader knows what Jesus' contemporaries can only wonder about.

We next encounter

> a rich lode of eschatological and messianic allusions embedded in the descriptive language of the narrative: in John's heraldry (in vv. 7f), in the associations evoked by John's appearance and behavior (in v. 6), in the opening reference to the prophet Isaiah, and in the conflate quote that follows it (in vv. 2f).[7]

Jesus emerges from the prophetic tradition.

The prophets were uncompromising advocates of the covenant, painfully aware of the disparity that existed, insistent that the people must repent, and confident of God's willingness to forgive. Jesus would be no less so. His heroic character begins to take shape.

While Jesus appears within the prophetic tradition (cf. 6:1), He also transcends it. John allows that he is not worthy to stoop down and untie Jesus' sandals (1:7). Whereas he had come baptizing with water, the Anointed would baptize with the Holy Spirit.

The tragic hero was thought to stand head and shoulders above the rest of humanity. He would evoke such as a classic passage from Ernest Renan:

> Mankind in its totality offers an assemblage of low beings, selfish, and superior to the animal only in that its selfishness is more reflective. From the midst of this uniform mediocrity there are pillars that rise towards the sky, and bear witness to a nobler destiny. Jesus is the highest of these pillars which show to man whence he comes, and whither he ought to tend.[8]

"Whatever may be the unexpected phenomena of the future," Renan concludes, "Jesus will not be surpassed. His worship will constantly renew its youth, the tale of his life will cause ceaseless tears, his sufferings will soften the best hearts; all the ages will proclaim that among

the sons of men there is none born who is greater than Jesus."
Paul Kirsch assumes a contrasting perspective.

> It is striking that Akiba's identification of Bar Cochba as Messiah, mistaken though it must be judged to have been, did not discredit Akiba himself. His prestige as an innovator and a shaper of Jewish sacred tradition could not be greater than it is. ...He evidently had hold of the normative Jewish notion of the Messiah, the "son of David" who sets this world straight by militarily and politically overthrowing tyranny and exploitation.[9]

Kirsch imagines that if Akiba had been a contemporary of Jesus, he would have "loved him dearly as a great teacher with a sure grasp of what was central," but not the Messiah as generally understood. Not all Jews would have agreed. As reported in Jewish circles, "where there are two Jews, there are at least three opinions."

Jesus could have sent His disciples ahead, blowing shofar and heralding His Messianic claims. This, coupled with His rapidly growing reputation, might have gathered Jewish zealots to throw off the tyranny of Rome. It would have accomplished little else, and but for a miraculous intervention hasten the Roman carnage.

He chose instead to employ the Jewish pedagogical technique of *solicited inquiry*. He acted so that the disciples asked one another: "Who is this? Even the winds and the waves obey him!" (4:41). They discarded alternative answers as inappropriate, while the true answer burned its way into their collective consciousness. Peter would eventually affirm their corporate conviction: "You are the Christ" (8:29). Even then, Jesus would warn him not to speak openly of their conviction. It would serve no good purpose.

The Son Of God

Whether we choose to include the contested phrase "the Son of God" (1:1) or not is inconsequential. The voice from heaven declared that "You are my Son, whom I love" (1:11). The demons prostrated themselves and cried out: "You are the Son of God" (3:11). Taken before the Sanhedrin, Jesus was condemned for acknowledging to be "the Son of the Blessed One" (14:61). Mark did not intend to leave the matter in doubt.

"Of all ancient peoples, the Hebrews were most surely possessed of the tragic sense of life. It pervades their ancient writings to an extent not true of the Greeks."[10] Thus when we turn to Hebrew tradition by way of understanding Jesus as the Son of God, we are well within the realm of tragedy.

We discover several Biblical referents to the sons of God. Otherwise stated, they form a *complex profile*.

Angels are sometimes referred to as sons of God (Job 1:6; 2:1; 38:7; Dan. 3:25). As such, they enjoy God's presence, consult with Him, and carry out His directives.

Although characteristically good, angels can and sometimes do fall from grace. In their fallen state, they are designated as demons.

Persons also can in an indiscriminate sense be called the sons of God. Thus Malachi inquires: "Have we not all one Father? Did not one God create us?" (2:10). If sons of God, then we should be obedient; if sons of God, then we ought to be concerned for our fellowman.

"Therefore since we are God's offspring," Paul reasoned, "we should not think that the divine being is like gold or silver or stone--an image made by man's design and skill" (Acts 17:29). "For if men are like God, it follows that an inanimate object cannot portray the living God; if men possess the spirit of God, they must surely recognize that God is Spirit and not capable of material representation."[11]

In a more particular sense, the Israelites were singled out as the sons of God. "You are the children of the Lord your God," Moses solemnly declared (Deut. 14:1). Keep the covenant stipulations and prosper. Fail to do so, and you will invite God's wrath.

The prophets picked up the refrain. "How gladly would I treat you like sons and give you a desirable land, the most beautiful inheritance of any nation. I thought you would call me 'Father' and not turn away from following me" (Jer. 3:19). "In the place where it was said to them, 'You are not my people,' they will be called 'sons of the living God'" (Hos. 1:10).

In a less restrictive sense, any righteous person might be called a son of God. This was the probable intent when the sons of God were said to cohabit with the daughters of men (Gen. 6:4). Their virtue and witness were compromised by being unequally yoked in marriage.

The designation is also used of a theocratic ruler. Thus we read: "You are my Son; today I have become your Father" (Psa. 2:7). "Today" likely refers to the time of coronation. It marks the occasion when the sovereign took upon himself the rights and privileges of office.

From this point on, he would be expected faithfully to fulfill his obligations as steward-ruler. He must promote the covenant ideals, and plead the case of his people before a merciful God. He also must exemplify the virtue demanded of his people as a whole.

Paul links the above text for Messianic purposes with another: "I will give you the holy and sure blessings promised to David" (Acts 13:33-34; cf. Isa. 55:3). As an earnest of this confidence, he cites Jesus' resurrection.

"You are my Son, whom I love; with you I am well pleased" (Mark 1:11).

> *You are my Son* echoes Psalm 2:7, a psalm originally addressed to the ancient Jewish kings. A son *whom I love* echoes Genesis 22:2, where God addresses Abraham, telling him to offer his son ("your only son, Isaac, whom you love"). *With you I am well pleased* reflects Isaiah 42:1, where God points to his servant as one chosen to speak for him.[12]

It also opens the door a crack for us to catch a glimpse of the solitary splendor of Jesus as the Father's one and only Son. Most obvious in this connection, Jesus *was sent by His Father*. As reminded by the eminent theologian Karl Barth, God does not ask us to cast ballots.

"*Abba*, Father," Jesus prayed, "everything is possible for you. Take this cup from me. Yet not what I will, but what you will" (14:36). Having received His salvic mission, He was determined to fulfill it despite the cost.

Also evident, Jesus *pleases and is beloved by His Father*. We recall a prophetic text: "Here is my servant, whom I uphold, my chosen one in whom I delight" (Isa. 42:1; cf. Matt. 12:18). At the transfiguration, a voice from the cloud confirms: "This is my Son whom I love" (Mark 9:7).

Not to be overlooked, Jesus *relies on the Father*. "By myself I can do nothing," Jesus allowed (John 5:19). As would an apprentice, He learned by example and imitation. He draws direction from His Father.

This recalls Gamaliel's sage advice to the Sanhedrin: "Leave these men alone! Let them go! For if their purpose or activity is of human origin, it will fail. But if it is from God, you will not be able to stop these men; you will only find yourselves fighting against God" (Acts 5:38-39).

Of crucial importance to the gospel accounts, Jesus reveals *His Father*. "Like father, like son," according to a traditional proverb.

"Lord, show us the Father and that will be enough for us," Philip implored Jesus (John 14:8). This he spoke to rephrase the question: "Where are you going?" Jesus answered: "Don't you know me, Philip, even after I have been among you such a long time? Anyone who has seen me has seen the Father." He had given material expression to a spiritual reality.

All things considered, Jesus *was one with His Father*. They were in mysterious fashion bonded together.

Mark does not explore this bondedness in theoretical fashion. He instead displays it for all to see. He wants us to observe and ponder what sort of person can still our turbulent emotions as readily as the winds and waves.

One wonders how this theme played to Mark's Gentile audience. They were accustomed to think of a son of God in mythological terms, via cohabitation of a god with human partner. Or in political connections, bestowing the term on a magistrate or general. Or in general, describing persons with exceptional qualities.

No doubt it differed from person to person. Some would make the transition easier than others.

Jesus employs sons of God in a final connection, concerning His disciples. "And when you stand praying, if you hold anything against anyone, forgive him, so that your Father in heaven may forgive your sins" (11:26). He links "My Father and your Father" as if to suggest a privileged relationship resulting from being in Christ (cf. John 20:17). Jesus instructs them to pray to *our* Father for *their* needs as *His* disciples.

Since the father in Semitic thinking is primarily an authority figure, we expect the son to be obedient. Thus while people may fall far short of the ideal, we expect the hero to respond on cue. Mark suggests that Jesus played His filial role to perfection.

Son of Man

Jesus preferred to designate Himself as the enigmatic *Son of Man* for reasons we can only surmise. The *complication* records two such instances. First of the two, persons brought a paralytic to Jesus for healing. Perceiving their faith, He said to the paralytic: "Son, your sins are forgiven you" (2:5).

Certain of the teachers of the law thought: "Why does this fellow talk like that? He is blaspheming! Who can forgive sins, but God alone?"

"Which is easier: to say to the paralytic, 'Your sins are forgiven,' or to say 'Get up, take your mat and walk'? But that you may know that the *Son of Man* has authority on earth to forgive sins," Jesus' voice trailed off. Turning to the infirmed, He instructed him to pick up his mat and go home.

This amazed everyone, soliciting their praise of God--who in Hebrew thought heals regardless of the means He chooses to employ. "We have never seen anything like this!" they concluded.

The second instance occurred as Jesus and His disciples were walking through a grain field on the Sabbath. Feeling the need for nourishment, the disciples picked some grain to satisfy their need. "Look," remonstrated certain Pharisees, "why are they doing what is unlawful on the Sabbath?" (2:24). Drawing upon a precedent set by David, Jesus concluded that "the Sabbath was made for man, not man for the Sabbath. So the *Son of Man* is Lord even of the Sabbath."

Jesus' response seems calculated to challenge the Pharisee's practice of applying Scripture as convenient. It also gave priority to human need over legal observance.

As for the Pharisees, they were perhaps not sure how to take Jesus' comments. Some would no doubt have put better construction on them than others. It would take time for them to sort things out in keeping with their agenda.

It does not serve the design of the *complication* to introduce too much too soon. A little here, a little there, and the weave begins to make itself evident.

Even so, the Son of Man is said to be the Lord of the Sabbath by way of the Sabbath being made for man. The argument is obscure, but not lost if we turn elsewhere for help.

The author of Hebrews observes that while we do not see all things subject to man, we see Jesus (as ideal man) exalted over all things (2:8-9). Jesus, reminiscent of the tragic hero paradigm, reflects the nobility with which we were endowed and before our free fall into depravity.

As such, Jesus gains an advantage point by which He can view life in proper perspective. With such, He can guide others as they negotiate life.

Jesus will later comment on the apocalyptic appearing of the Son of Man. "At that time men will see the Son of Man coming in clouds with great power and glory" (13:26). At this, "he will send his angels and gather his elect from the four winds, from the ends of the earth to the ends of the heavens."

The text recalls Daniel's vision of "one like the son of man coming in the clouds of heaven" (7:13). While most scholars take this to be a corporate reference, given the nature of corporate personality--the focus can readily shift back and forth between the collective and a representative individual.

Less to the disciples' liking, Jesus would "teach them that the Son of Man must suffer many things and be rejected by the elders, chief priests and teachers of the law, and that he must be killed and after three days rise again" (8:31). When Peter vigorously protested, Jesus remained resolute: "If anyone is ashamed of me and my words in this adulterous and sinful generation, the Son of Man will be ashamed of him when he comes in his Father's glory with the holy angels."

This clearly recalls Isaiah's description of the Suffering Servant: "He was despised and rejected by men, a man of sorrows, and familiar with suffering" (53:3). "But he was pierced for our transgressions, he was crushed for our iniquities; the punishment that brought us peace was upon him, and by his wounds we are healed."

Out of the depths, we cry for deliverance. Up from the depths, He would deliver us. Expectantly into the future, He would guide us. Thus the tragic hero snatches spiritual victory out of seeming defeat.

As eulogized by Philip Bliss: 'Man of Sorrows', what a name for the Son of God, who came ruined sinners to reclaim! Hallelujah! what a Saviour! When He comes, our glorious King, all His ransomed home to bring, then anew this song we'll sing: Hallelujah! what a Saviour!"

Chapter 2

TRAGIC FLAW

In classic tragedy, the hero falls prey to *harmatia*, an error in judgment commonly expressed as a *flaw*. Such as when too confident, he disregards a divine oracle. This predictably results in his undoing.

At first glance, we might think this inappropriate for Mark's hero. Upon further reflection, it proves to be dead on target.

Flaw in Focus

"There are certainly tragic heroes who possess flaws," Walter Kerr allows. "There are tragic heroes who seem in some way flawed, though we have great difficulty in saying just what has flawed them. And there are tragic heroes who seem altogether unstained but suffer nonetheless."[13] Mark represents Jesus while afflicted by men approved by God.

Kerr comments further: "Given the goodness of the goal and the exceptional powers of the man pursuing it, the puzzle of tragedy is that its heroes should ever fail. On the face of things, the odds would seem to favor success."[14] Unless, of course, there were some mitigating factor. Such as might resemble a satellite invisible to the naked eye but creating an irregular course around the planet it orbits.

Mark subtly explores the problem by drawing our attention to the wilderness. Scripture characterizes it as "a land where no man lives" (Job 26). It is dry, desolate, sparsely settled or altogether unfit for human dwelling.

Mark associates the wilderness with austerity, repentance, inauguration, and temptation. John's clothing and diet were those of the wilderness nomad, emphasizing the austere character of his life. They also recall Elijah, whose return was to precede the Messiah (2 Kings 1:8; Mal. 4:5-6). John was not explicitly identified with Elijah until a later time (9:12-13).

Austerity reminds us of the pilgrim character of life. This world is not our home; we are just passing through. As illustrated by the Hebrew people, we are pressing on toward the promised land. Whatever advantages the wilderness may have to offer, we ought not to linger there longer than necessary.

"John's call to repentance and his call to come out to him in the wilderness to be baptized are two aspects of the same reality. It is a call to renew sonship in the wilderness."[15] The matter takes on special urgency since it coincides with the curtain rising on the final act of God's redemptive drama.

Repentance implies a change of disposition resulting in forgiveness. Thus Jeremiah cautioned: "Now reform your ways and your actions and obey the Lord your God. Then the Lord will relent and not bring the disaster he has pronounced against you" (26:13). If not, their guilt would remain. "At that time Jesus came from Nazareth in Galilee and was baptized by John in the Jordan" (1:9). Mark does not elaborate except to note that the Spirit descended on him like a dove, and a voice from heaven declared Him to be "my Son, whom I love" and with whom "I am well pleased." Even so, this would suggest that Jesus was blameless.

Matthew reports that John concurred, and that Jesus insisted so as "to fulfill all righteousness" (3:14-15). That is to say, to fulfill God's purpose for His life. Why, then, was it God's will that Jesus be baptized? Likely to identify with those He came to save, signal the beginning (*inauguration*) of His salvic ministry, and anticipate His vicarious death.

"At once the Spirit sent him out into the desert, and he was in the desert forty days, being tempted by Satan" (1:12). "In the fuller account of the *temptation* given in the other gospels, it is made clear that the purpose of this wilderness period was that Jesus might face and conquer the peculiar temptations involved in His calling as Messiah before commencing His task. Again, Mark is clipped and direct."[16]

As Mark's narrative unfolds, his intent becomes clear. Whereas Israel failed its probation in the wilderness, Christ succeeded.

Mark's perception of Jesus' *flaw* seems unmistakable. Where some tragic heroes clearly are flawed, Jesus was not one of these. Where some imperceptibly are flawed, Jesus was not among them. Where some suffered because of circumstances voluntarily assumed, Jesus served as a prime case in point.

Flaw Expounded

Chaos theory provides us with a helpful framework for understanding flaw as applied to Mark's tragic hero. It also recalls the Biblical emphasis on chaos. We will touch on the former before turning in greater detail to the latter.

The weather defies

> long-range prediction because it is too sensitive to almost imperceptible changes in the initial condition, which changes lead to slightly bigger ones a minute later or a foot away, which slightly bigger ones lead to yet more substantial deviations, the whole process cascading over time into a nonrepetitive unpredictability.[17]

We describe such conditions as chaotic.

> If you watch from a bridge as a leaf floats down a stream, you may see it trapped by a small whirlpool, circulate a few times, and escape, only to be trapped again further down the stream. Trying to guess what will happen to a leaf as it comes into view from under the bridge is an idle pursuit in more senses than one: the tiniest shift in the leaf's position can completely change its future course.[18]

Such is the trademark of chaos.

From chaos perspective, order gives way to chaos and chaos to order. The more things appear different, the more certain things appear constant.

"Now the earth was formless and empty, darkness was over the surface of the deep, and the Spirit of God was hovering over the waters" (Gen. 1:2). We find the phrase "formless and empty" only here and concerning impending destruction (Jer. 4:23).

While not inviting, primeval chaos was only the first stage of God's creative activity. It resembles the potter's clay stacked in preparation for casting a vessel.

As the Biblical narrative unfolds, the word of God came to Jeremiah, instructing him to go to the potter's house (18:1). At this, he observed that the pot when marred was recast into another. "Like clay in the hand of the potter," God declared, "so are you in my hand, O house of Israel."

Subsequent experience with chaos exceeds its original expression. First, it suggests that something has gone wrong. "Yet my people have forgotten me; they burn incense to worthless idols, which made them stumble in their ways and in the ancient paths."

Second, it alerts us of God's wrath. If a people "does evil in my sight and does not obey me, then I will reconsider the good I had intended to do for it."

Third, it urges us to repent in anticipation of God's forgiveness and restoration. "So turn from evil ways and your actions." Turn and live!

Historical chaos can be illustrated over and again. We will sketch only the experience of Job, before returning to Mark's narrative. Job was a good man, who feared God and shunned evil. He was so wealthy as to have no peer "among all the people of the East" (1:3).

Then, chaos set in with dramatic suddenness. A messenger brought him word that the Sabeans had attacked and carried off his oxen and donkeys, and put his servants to the sword. "While he was still speaking," another arrived with the report that fire had fallen from heaven burning up his sheep and servants; "while he was still speaking," still another announced that three Chaldean raiding parties had driven off his camels; "while he was still speaking," a final messenger informed him that a mighty wind had collapsed the house where his children were feasting and all were dead.

Job's first reaction was to rend his garment and shave his head, as signs of mourning. "Naked I came from my mother's womb, and naked I will depart," he consoled himself. "The Lord gave and the Lord has taken away; may the Lord be praised" (1:21). At which the writer appreciatively observes: "In all this, Job did not sin by charging God with wrongdoing."

Several thousand words later, God also commended the patriarch. After which we read that the "Lord blessed the latter part of Job's life more than the first" (42:12). As order had given way to chaos, so chaos to order.

The people continued to ignore the prophets until at long last their warning ceased. It was as if the heavens had turned to brass.

The silent years were not uneventful. As in the times of the judges, each followed his personal agenda. Matters were in disarray.

Mark succinctly announced a new beginning (1:1), corresponding to its antecedent (Gen. 1:1). The gospel might be understood as an evangelical extension of creation.

The parallel extends with John's prophetic call to prepare the way of the Lord (1:3). Where once God broke the primeval silence to bring order out of chaos, so now John broke prophetic silence to usher in the new age.

Chaos continues to manifest itself in various ways, such as Jesus' confrontation with evil spirits. He was tempted, as was Adam before

Him, but withstood the test (1:12-13). He thus qualified as *a wilderness person* like Moses and Elijah before Him. That is to say, He was one tried and proved in the crucible of chaos.

"What do you want of us, Jesus of Nazareth," cried out a demon. "I know who you are--the Holy One of God!" (1:24; cf. 3:11; 5:7). "The recognition-formula is not a confession, but a defensive attempt to gain control of Jesus in accordance with the common concept of that day, that the use of the precise name of an individual or spirit would secure mastery over him."[19] Failing in its attempt, the demon was driven out.

The ordinary sick folk responded in less precise terms: "Lord" (7:8), "Teacher" (9:17), "Son of David" (10:47-48), or "Master" (10:51). They had reached the end of their rope, and reached for a helping hand.

"As for man, his days are like grass, he flourishes like a flower of the field; the wind blows over it and it is gone, and its place remembers it no more" (Psa. 103:15). He resembles the wilderness flowers in spring time, before the scorching wind leaves the slopes bare. Such is life before sickness and death claim their victim. Order out of chaos, and chaos from order.

A final illustration will suffice. Jesus was in the stern of the boat, fast asleep when a furious squall came up (4:35). Unperturbed, He slept on. "Teacher, don't you care if we drown?" shouted the desperate disciples to make themselves heard above the howling winds. Jesus, rousing Himself, rebuked the elements so that "the wind died down and it was completely calm."

The cosmic overtones are apparent. God remains sovereign over creation and history. Where once He brought order out of chaos with the creation, so now He holds back the return of chaos.

Jesus turns pointedly to the disciples: "Why are you so afraid? Do you still have no faith?" They differ from the multitude at this point only in degree.

Once, countless generations ago, humanity had become so evil that God would no longer put up with it (Gen. 6:13). Having secured righteous Noah and his family, He allowed chaos to ravage as a great flood. When the waters had subsided, God promised never again to visit the world with so complete a destruction. Since then chaos has been on a shorter leash, however distressing it may appear.

Flaw "Exploited"

Mark emphasizes that we should not despair of life because it is flawed. Quite the reverse! We can by God's grace turn obstacles into opportunities.

Levi was a tax collector.

> Such officials were detested everywhere and were classed with the vilest of men (i.e., with robbers and murderers). The practice of leasing the customs duty of a district at a fixed sum encouraged gross oppression by tax officers anxious to secure as large a profit as possible. When a Jew entered the customs service he was regarded as an outcast from society: he was disqualified as a judge or a witness in a court session, was excommunicated from the synagogue, and in the eyes of the community his disgrace extended to his family.[20]

He had made his bed, and now must sleep on it--according to traditional wisdom, but the narrative takes an unexpected turn. "Follow me" Jesus invited, and Levi resolutely responded (2:14). When others protested, Jesus remonstrated: "It is not the healthy who need a doctor, but the sick. I have not come to call the righteous, but sinners."

What must have appeared as an insurmountable obstacle, provided the necessary incentive. Levi threw caution to the wind, and seized his opportunity. Others simply expressed their disapproval and continued to flounder.

Some time later, Jesus retired to a solitary place only to discover that the people had proceeded Him. They listened intently to His teaching until the day was spent. Upon which, Jesus' disciples urged Him to send the multitude away so that they could secure food in the surrounding villages.

Jesus insisted: "You give them something to eat" (6:37). "That would take eight months of a man's wages!" they gasped in astonishment.

"How many loaves do you have?" Jesus insisted. "Go and see." They reported back: "Five and two fish."

Jesus instructed them to sit the people in groups, and when He had given thanks to distribute the food. There proved to be more than enough for all. With God a little goes an amazingly long way.

Such examples were not intended to illustrate the power of positive thinking. Man makes a poor savior.

Mark instead wants to call our attention to Jesus. As the martyr theologian Dietrich Bonhoeffer liked to affirm, Jesus stands where we cannot and stands there for us. Mark makes no claim for himself, but reports the gospel of "Jesus Christ, the Son of God."

As for the disciples, this had yet to sink in. Mark observes that "they had not understood about the loaves; their hearts were hardened" (6:52). The *crises* remained future; the *complication* must first run its course.

Even so, anticipation builds with each passing episode. Eventually the reality will break through. If not for all, then for some.

As for now, savor the moment. Sense the ambiguity that pervades life, the bias that thwarts it, and the grace that releases it. Give God time to do His perfect work through Christ and on our behalf.

Chapter 3

TRAGIC DESIGN

"In its origin, ancient tragedy was essentially religious."[21] Mark is clearly no exception.

"The time has come," Jesus declared. "The kingdom of God is near. Repent and believe the good news!" (1:15). While His message had profound personal and social implications, it was primarily religious in character.

Gentiles, unlike their Jewish counterpart, were for the most part unfamiliar with the prophetic tradition. Instead, they could draw upon such High God traditions as were familiar to them. It was in this context that they would have understood the demoniac's query: "What do you want with me, Son of the Most High God?" (5:7).

The Most High God

"The term *high god* or *supreme god* is usually applied to the deity that outranks all others; the same terms are used in monotheism, where there is only one god."[22] The consensus High God reveals similar traits whether in monotheistic or polytheistic context.

Wilhelm Schmidt provided us with a comprehensive understanding of the High God traditions that has stood the test of time. He proposed as attributes of the Supreme God: eternity (primordial), omniscience, beneficence, morality, omnipotence, and creative power. We will touch on these in order before easing back into Mark's narrative. "A sort of eternity is ascribed to all these Supreme Beings more or less clearly, whenever we have anything like detailed information. The form of the statements is that they existed before all other beings, have always been and always will be, or that they never die."[23] The traditions commonly suggest that He is before all things, and involved with their coming into being. Less frequently they suggest that He has always been or always will be.

The term *primordial* seems better to fit the data than Schmidt's obscure reference to "a sort of eternity." As illustrated by the Genesis' account, "In the beginning God created the heavens and the earth" (1:1).

The resiliency of the High God tradition in Greek culture seems reflected in Paul's reference to an *Unknown God*, which he discussed in traditional fashion. His audience appears to have taken his discourse in stride until he mentions the resurrection, which runs counter to their view of immortality (Acts 17:22-32).

The Batwa of Rwanda assert that "there is nothing which Imanai does not know about; he knows everything." He is omniscient.

The Batek Nogu observe that "Keto's eyes are the sun and moon," to which the Samayeds add that "the stars are God's ears." He is omniscient.

If God is omniscient, we cannot hope to hide our sins from Him. "You have set our iniquities before you," the psalmist observed, "our secret sins in the light of your presence" (90:8).

The *Iroquois Constitution* mandated that each council was to invoke the messengers of "the Great Spirit who dwells in the skies above, who gives all things useful to me, who is the source and the ruler of health and life." They were to solicit the guidance of those spirits that serve a benevolent sovereign.

The Ewe report that "He is good, for He has never withdrawn from us the good things which He gave us." "One generation will commend your works to another; they will tell of your mighty acts" (Psa. 145:4).

The High God is without qualification righteous. He established the moral law that judges us; He commends those who act properly; He abhors and punishes those who offend. "The fear of the Lord is pure, enduring forever. The ordinances of the Lord are sure and altogether righteous" (Psa. 19:9). They are more precious than gold, and sweeter than honey.

To contrast God's righteousness with the evil we experience, some traditions posit an evil adversary to account for this disparity. It is not, as Schmidt reminds us, a proper dualism "for the Supreme Being is represented as far the stronger and more important."

In fact, the High God is omnipotent. The Barotze address Him as "the Great King," who is sovereign over all. The Akan refer to Him as ruler of the sky, earth, and underworld.

Tragic Design 91

"Seven times will pass by for you until you acknowledge that the Most High is sovereign over the kingdoms of men and gives them to anyone he wishes," Daniel warned Nebuchadnezzar (4:25). The king, once humbled, confessed that "He does as he pleases with the powers of heaven and the peoples of the earth. No one can hold back his hand" (v. 35).

The High God's power is evident from creation, and by extension with His preservation and providence. The potter motif, as earlier illustrated, is common in the traditions. There are exceptions, as with the Adamba, who suggest that the High God first whittled creation to a manageable size, and then worked out the finer detail.

> It must be remembered that for many African peoples, God's active part in human history is seen in terms of His supplying them with rain, good harvest, health, cattle and children; in healing, delivering and helping them; and in terms of making His presence felt through natural phenomena and objects.[24]

He works with what is available to provide what we need. "The Lord is my shepherd, I shall not be in want" (Psa. 23:1).

All this considered, Jesus announced the kingdom of God as drawing near. For those relying primarily on High God traditions, this would minimally imply a divine initiative. The demonic forces would be thrown into retreat, along with the oppressive features of society. Righteousness would be rewarded.

Jesus is put to the test. As noted earlier, a demon hopes to control Jesus by use of His name. To no avail! Jesus put the demon to flight.

The religious establishment, portrayed as an oppressive institution, charged that "by the prince of demons he is driving out demons" (3:22). Jesus impuned their logic: "If a house is divided against itself, that house cannot stand. ...In fact, no one can enter a strong man's house and carry off his possessions unless he first ties up the strong man."

As another evidence for His claims, Jesus healed the physically infirm. In one especially dramatic instance, a large crowd was pressing in on Him. A woman who had exhausted her savings in a futile effort to be cured, reached out to touch Jesus' cloak. She reasoned "if I just touch his clothes, I will be healed" (5:28). Immediately she was made well.

Jesus turned to inquire "who has touched my clothes?" "You see the people crowding against you," his disciples responded, "and yet you ask 'Who touched me?'" Unimpressed, Jesus continued to look about. At which the woman confessed what had happened. "Your faith (rather than some miraculous quality of the garment) has healed you," Jesus concluded.

Jesus told a series of parables to illustrate how God's will would be realized. It resembles a farmer planting seed. "Some people are like seed along the path, where the word is sown. As soon as they hear it, Satan comes and takes away the word that was sown in them" (4:15). Others resemble seed sown on rocky places, who have no root and flourish briefly. Still others remind us of seed sown among thorns, so that other concerns take precedent. Finally, some seed fall on good ground, and bring forth fruit--"thirty, sixty, or even a hundred times what was sown."

Consider also how a plant grows. "All by itself the soil produces grain--first the stalk, then the head, then the full kernel in the head" (4:28). We are responsible only for sowing the seed; God provides the increase (cf. 1 Cor. 3:6).

Do not judge the result by its modest beginning. The kingdom resembles a mustard seed, smallest of those we plant in the garden but growing larger than the rest (4:31-32).

In these and other ways, Jesus assured His hearers concerning the "good news of God" (1:14). This was, as expressed in a textual variant, the "good news of the kingdom." Qualifications aside, God's will would be done on earth as it was in heaven.

In Covenant Perspective

Jesus' Jewish audience had a distinct advantage when it came to understanding His kingdom proclamation. They enjoyed the legacy of the prophets. We will consider first a prophetic understanding of the kingdom, followed by Jesus' refinement as Mark records it.

> While the idiom "the Kingdom of God" does not occur in the Old Testament, the idea is found throughout the prophets. There is a twofold emphasis on God's kingship. He is frequently spoken of as the King, both of Israel (Exod. 15:18; Deut. 33:5) and of all the earth (Psa. 29:10; Isa. 6:5). Although God is now King, other references speak of a day when he shall become King (Isa. 24:23: Zech. 3:15).[25]

Three distinct although related contexts are involved.

First, God is sovereign over all creation. "The kings of the earth take their stand and the rulers gather together against the Lord and against his Anointed One" (Psa. 2:2). They resemble so many Lilliputians, beating their shields as if to frighten the Almighty.

"The One enthroned in heaven laughs; the Lord scoffs at them. Then he rebukes them in his anger and terrifies them in his wrath." They were no match for Him. His sovereign reign remained secure.

Isaiah emphatically concurs. "He stretches out the heavens like a canopy, and spreads them out like a tent to live in. He brings princes to naught and reduces the rulers of this world to nothing" (40:22).

Second, the kingdom of God is associated with the covenant people. God established a covenant (vassal treaty) relationship with the Hebrews. He would be their Sovereign (*Suzerain*), and they His subjects.

Balaam therefore concluded "the Lord their God is with them; the shout of the King is among them" (Num. 23:21). Isaiah reminds the chosen of the Almighty's pledge to them: "I am the Lord, your Holy One, Israel's Creator, your King" (Isa. 43:10).

This theocratic ideal was carried over with the monarchy as fine-tuned by the prophets. "What more can David say to you? For you know your servant, O Sovereign Lord. For the sake of your word and according to your will, you have done this great thing and made it known to your servant" (2 Sam. 7:20-21). "'Return, faithless Israel,' declares the Lord, 'I will frown on you no longer, for I am merciful,' declares the Lord" (Jer. 3:12).

Third, the kingdom ideal was relegated to the future. "How beautiful on the mountains are the feet of those who bring good news, who proclaim peace, who bring good tidings, who proclaim salvation, who say to Zion, 'Your God reigns!'" (Isa. 52:7).

"The time has come," Jesus announced. "The kingdom of God is near" (1:15).

> The emphasis on the fullness of time grounds Jesus' proclamation securely in the history of revelation and redemption. It focuses on the God who acts, whose past election and redemption of Israel provided the pledge for his activity in the future. Jesus declares that the critical moment has come: God begins to act in a new and decisive way, bringing his promise of ultimate redemption to the point of fulfillment.[26]

Mark elaborates the theme in four connections: with Jesus, His disciples, the world at large, and the consummation. Jesus incarnates the kingdom. He was God's will personified.

As such, Jesus expressed the confident trust that a child extends to its father. As such, He retained an openness to others and their needs. "Finally, Jesus lived with a definite sense of purpose for his life and with an energy that defies imitation."[27]

He bid others to follow Him. As Jesus was walking by the sea, He saw Simon and his brother Andrew casting a net into the lake. "Come, follow me," Jesus said, "and I will make you fishers of men" (1:17). Walking on a bit further, He saw James the son of Zebedee and his brother John in a boat, preparing their nets. "Without delay he called them, and they left their father Zebedee in the boat with the hired men and followed him."

It was in response to Jesus' call rather than any explicit considerations that the disciples responded. Their willingness to follow *Him* involved "responding to a summons, attachment to a person, acceptance of authority, and imitation of example. The implication of continuation and pursuing a goal also is included."[28]

The demand was always the same. Regardless of what specifically they left to follow Jesus, it was all. Despite what it subsequently demanded, it was everything.

As a result, the kingdom focus increased beyond Jesus to embrace His disciples. They would together bear witness to kingdom priorities.

Jesus did not limit the arrival of the kingdom to the community of faith. It would impact on the world at large. "In relationship to the political structures of Palestine under Roman occupation, Jesus neither advocated a passive acceptance nor a violent resistance. The proclamation of the Kingdom of God was not directly a political program."[29] Its influence was expressed indirectly: through Jesus being in their midst, through His teaching, and with the community He left behind.

The kingdom acts as a social catalyst, affecting how other elements relate but not itself altered. Jesus described it as pouring new wine into an old wineskin (2:22). He intended to illustrate how inappropriate old ways were to the new situation.

We can appreciate how difficult this was for the political, social, and religious establishments. They had invested interest in sustaining the status quo. Jesus appeared as a threat, if only in one regard then in all.

Jesus urges persons to let go and get in the kingdom flow. Lose your life and find it.

The *complication* focuses our attention of the contemporary significance of the kingdom. The *not yet* aspect of the kingdom remains for later consideration (cf. 13:1-31). The kingdom *has* come as an earnest; the kingdom *will* come in its fullness. One can live toward the future, but not indefinitely cling to the past.

This recalls an incident with which we will conclude. Jesus' mother

Tragic Design

and brothers had arrived, and sent for Him. He took this opportunity to inquire: "Who are my mother and my brothers?" (3:31). "Then he looked at those seated in a circle around him and said, 'Here are my mother and my brothers! Whoever does God's will is my brother and sister and mother.'"

Jesus left the circle open so that others might join. He did not restrict it to family or by any other consideration except willingness to do God's will. God's will be done was and is the kingdom imperative.

Chapter 4

TRAGIC CONSEQUENCE

With this topic, we draw Mark's *complication* to a close. We have considered in order his tragic hero, tragic flaw, and tragic design.

It remains to sketch his tragic consequence. This will provide us with a key to understanding life as we experience it. We will sense something of the high ideals that beckon, the problems that inhibit, and the prospect open to us. We find ourselves identifying with the various characters as they are introduced, speak their lines, and walk off the stage. We humans, after all has been said, are cut from the same piece of cloth.

Natural Characteristics

We ought not to overlook the obvious. Mark presupposes the use of language. He also illustrates its usefulness and limitations.

"Be quiet!" Jesus rebuked the demon who bore witness of Him (1:25); "Let us go somewhere else," He urged the disciples, "so I can preach there also" (1:38). He said to the paralytic: "Son, your sins are forgiven" (2:6).

As in the last instance, this sometimes created confusion and controversy. Jesus' protagonists thought He had committed blasphemy. Jesus replied that He had thus spoken so that "You may know that the Son of Man has authority on earth to forgive sins" (v. 10).

The interchange resembles the tip of an iceberg. Much remains undisclosed and readily misunderstood.

It appears that some turned Him off at this point; their minds were made up. Others would hear Him out; they were willing to be convinced. Still others would take their cue from someone else; they would shift to the way the wind was blowing.

Language is an extremely complex form of communication. Said to have thirteen features, we follow Peoples and Bailey in limiting our discussion to five. First, it employs multiple means. "Ordinarily, language messages are spoken (the medium is sound), but they may also be written or signed with movements of the hand. Humans can even send language messages through touch."[30]

Second, it relies on largely arbitrary symbols. Paul Tillich used to distinguish between symbols that were not altogether arbitrary and those that are. Illustrative of the former, water conveys the idea of cleansing in Baptism; illustrative of the latter, there seems nothing about a red light to signify that we stop--except perhaps that we can readily see it.

Third, it combines discreet elements to communicate meaning. "By mastering their language's lexicon, or its words and their meanings, and its syntax, or rules for combining words into sentences, speakers and hearers can send and receive messages of great complexity with amazing precision."[31]

Fourth, it can express novel ideas. It may break new ground, or tie together former material in creative fashion. In any case, it offers a building block for others to employ.

Finally, it exhibits *displacement*. That is, it allows us to talk about objects, people, and events far removed in time and space. These need not be actual, as with imaginary creatures of folk lore.

"The tongue also is a fire," James complains (3:6). We abuse others when we ought to edify them. We harm when we should help. The greater the gift, the more tragic its misuse.

Humans also are distinctive in the precision with which they fashion and use tools. Early on, Jesus encountered Simon and Andrew, James and John, engaged with their fishing vocation. The former were casting a net into the sea; the latter were preparing their nets. Jesus informed them that from this point on they would apply their skills to catching people.

Precision becomes comprehensive with the creation and maintenance of culture. Here we define *culture* in its broadest sense as a conventional way of life.

When Jesus reached out to touch a man with leprosy, He ignored a cultural prohibition meant to protect persons from contracting the disease (1:41). When Jesus called Levi to follow Him, He challenged a cultural prejudice concerning tax collectors and the irreligious (1:14). When Jesus insisted that He was Lord of the Sabbath, He repudiated the fence religious leaders had built to protect their flock (2:27-28).

In each of these instances, we can sense how refined skill can both serve and prove counterproductive. "The Sabbath is made for man," Jesus concluded, "not man for the Sabbath." If Sabbath serves man, then it fulfills a need; if man for the Sabbath, then it becomes an unnecessary burden.

Humans are also moral. They distinguish between right and wrong, even when their ideas of right and wrong differ.

It was a ghastly thing that befell John the Baptist. Cast into prison because of his fearless indictment of Herod's behavior, he was for a time spared due to his righteous reputation. Even this did not save him when the ruler felt obligated to honor his impetuous vow to Herodias' daughter (6:26-27).

It was a good thing when Jesus went throughout the region preaching the gospel, and healed many. Persons flocked to hear Him and benefit from His touch (1:5; 3:7; 7:37).

The moral dilemma, as Paul would describe it, is that what we want to do, we do not; and what we do not want to do, we do (cf. Rom. 7:15-16). Or to put the golden rule in reverse: we do not want others to do to us as we do to them.

Humans are finally religious. The fool who says in his heart that there is no God chooses to disregard Him, not deny His existence. The more we protest, the more it seems evident that man is incurably religious.

Jesus came preaching that the kingdom of God was near. It struck a familiar chord.

Jesus' message carried a sense of urgency. Other things could be postponed without serious consequences, but not the onrushing of the kingdom.

Religious issues predominated in Jesus' teaching. "And when you pray, do not keep on babbling like pagans, for they think they will be heard because of their many words" (6:7). Pray instead as a child would petition his father, assured of a sympathetic hearing.

Religious issues predominated in Jesus' controversies. "When you fast, do not look somber as the hypocrites do, for they disfigure their faces to show men they are fasting" (6:16). They already have their reward, having received it from men. But when you pray, do not let on to others, and "your Father, who sees what is done in secret, will reward you."

Man employs religion against God. He prefers idolatry to worship of the Almighty.

"You made him a little lower than the heavenly beings," the psalmist reflected on man's noble origin, "and crowned him with glory and honor.

You made him ruler over the works of your hands; you put everything under his feet" (8:5-6). We no longer view him as such. He seems unable to control himself, let alone manage creation for God. Some tragic development has intervened.

Acquired Characteristics

The culprit is sin. "The core of sin is unbelief, and its chief manifestations are pride, fear, and sloth. Sin is not simply concupiscence, the inclination to sin, but a lust for power. It is not so much a deficiency of the good as an assault on the good."[32] It involves not only an act of transgression, but a resulting state of estrangement.

Opposition arose first among the religious establishment. Unable to deny that Jesus performed miracles, it attributed them to Beelzebub--the prince of demons (3:22). It did not believe, nor did it want others to believe.

No doubt it felt its power over the people slipping away. Jesus was receiving attention once reserved for the religious elite, and attention they could never genuinely command.

Unbelief extended to Jesus' family and erstwhile friends. "Where did this man get these things?" they asked. "What's this wisdom that has been given him, that he even does miracles!" (6:2). Is this not the carpenter, and are not His siblings among us? As for Jesus, He "was amazed at their lack of faith."

Herod expresses the symptoms of sin more clearly than perhaps any other. He had married his brother Philip's wife in violation of the *Torah* (teaching, law). Rather than repent of his sin, he imprisoned John. Fearing John as "a righteous and holy man," he was reluctant to put him to death. Puzzled by John's words, he nonetheless enjoyed listening to him.

Herod prided himself for being in control. If he so desired, he could terminate John's life.

His power proved to be his undoing. Trapped by an impetuous pledge, he was caught in a bind. He had to execute John to keep face. Sin is master of all, and servant to none.

The disciples were no exception. "Why are you so afraid?" Jesus asked them. "Do you still have no faith?" (4:40). In a manner of speaking, they were sinners with a redemptive footnote.

On the other hand, the demoniacs were sinners with an exclamation mark. "Have you come to destroy us?" an evil spirit cried out to Jesus

(1:24). Sooner or later, he seems to assume this would be his fate. He had declared war on all that is good, and the warfare would continue until its bitter end.

Insecurity follows in the wake of sin. Persons hold desperately to whatever has helped them survive, as if to a piece of floating wreckage after the ship has capsized.

Jesus does not take their desperation lightly. He seems to sense when to press the issue, and when to hold back. He takes no pleasure in pushing them off a cliff.

"No one sews a patch of unshrunk cloth on an old garment," Jesus warned. "If he does, the new piece will pull away from the old, making the tear worse" (2:21). Nor does one pour new wine into old wineskins. "If he does, the wine will burst the skins, and both the wine and the wineskins will be ruined."

With these and other words, Jesus encouraged His listeners to break with the past and take on a new challenge. Have the courage to step forward in faith, while burning your bridges behind you.

Survival instincts more often take over. We drag our feet a little longer, hoping for the best. Until all too often we lose the God-given opportunity. Jesus passes us by on the way to another village, where the drama will be reenacted.

We also must contend with social pressure. "Lord, first let me go and bury my father," a would-be disciple requested (Matt. 8:21). Whatever his personal conviction, he would obviously conform to social expectation.

In contrast, James and John "left their father Zebedee in the boat with the hired men and followed him" (1:20). Social expectation to the contrary, they would follow Jesus.

Sometime later, Jesus' mother and brothers arrived. Standing outside, they sent for Him (3:31).

> In this passage the two groups who should have recognized Jesus first, his own family and the teachers of the law, are both blind to his true identity. Jesus' relatives respond out of concern for him and perhaps for the reputation of the family. The scribes from Jerusalem respond out of hostility, rejecting Jesus and his message.[33]

Both seek to bring social pressure to bear on Him. Neither succeeded.

Many waver when confronted with social resistance. "Like seed sown on rocky places, (they) hear the word and at once receive it with joy. But since they have no root, they last only a short time. When trouble or persecution comes because of the word, they quickly fall away" (4:16-17).

"Still others, like seed sown among thorns, hear the word; but the worries of this life, the deceitfulness of wealth and the desires for other things come in and choke the word, making it unfruitful" (vv. 18-19). They need to put kingdom priorities first in their lives, and other matters will fall into place.

Failing to do so, nothing will turn out right. The more they get, the more they want. The more they achieve, the less it will satisfy.

Thus far, we have painted a largely dismal portrait of humanity. Sin ravages life as hope takes flight.

Even so, there appears a counter theme running through the narrative. Here and there, now and then, we catch a glimpse of persons earnestly seeking religious reality. They are not for the most part those we think to be open to the good news, i.e., the religious leaders and others of standing in the community. More often than not, they appear as common folk or even social outcasts.

Mark distinguishes these from the multitude. Thus while the crowd jostled Jesus, only the woman bent on healing touched Him.

The way does not appear as if broad enough to accommodate a surge of the multitude. It allows for one person at a time, and those who embrace surpassing righteousness as a requirement for entrance into the kingdom of God.

The Syrophoenician woman provides a striking case in point (7:24-30). She came from an area Josephus describes as "notoriously our bitterest enemies" (*Apion 1.15*). Jesus had retired to the district for privacy, but was discovered.

The woman earnestly petitioned Jesus to exorcise her daughter. "First let the children eat all they want," Jesus responded, "for it is not right to take the children's bread and toss it to their dogs." Whatever the cause, Jesus rejected her appeal on the grounds of her being a Gentile.

Even so, a mark of faith is its insistence to see possibilities where there appear to be none. "Yes, Lord," she replied, "but even the dogs under the table eat the children's crumbs." Commending her response, Jesus honored her petition.

> Jesus' ministry did not exclude Gentiles entirely as the synoptic tradition indicates, but the Gentiles participated by receiving the "children's crumbs" through an act of faith in Jesus as the one sent to Israel. For Mark, however, this very participation became possible because of the ultimate thrust of Jesus' redemptive ministry that removed the social/ritual boundaries between Jew and Greek, clean and unclean.[34]

He deliberately laid the foundation of Gentile missions in His ministry to those shunned by society.

None are so privileged that they can take eternity for granted. Conversely, none are so disadvantaged that they should despair.

The *complication* has run its course with the tragic consequence of human transgression. We are left to reflect on our fallen condition. On the one hand, we are "fearfully and wonderfully made" (Psa. 139:14). On the other, we have squandered a Godly legacy.

We have met the enemy, and he is us. We cannot blame our dilemma on others.

We are not left to meditate on our failure. Guilt can be our undoing by stripping us of any incentive.

Mark instead calls our attention to Jesus and His message. "The time has come," He said. "The kingdom of God is near. Repent and believe the good news!" (1:15). This is not so much a way out and the way through an impasse. After this, Jesus will help us negotiate the tragic consequences of life in a fallen world.

Chapter 5

REALITY

"In the Aristotelian concept of plot structure, the transition between complication and denouement is called the crisis. At this point a climactic event takes place that results in a shift in the action for the play."[35] It often takes the form of a recognition scene, as in Mark's narrative.

Jesus asked His disciples: "Who do people say I am?" (8:27). "Some say John the Baptist; others say Elijah; and still others, one of the prophets," they replied. "But what about you?" Jesus persisted. "Who do you say I am?" Peter answered: "You are the Christ."

Flashback

Previously, this insight was reserved for Jesus, the demons, and Mark's audience. "Jesus, the demons, and the reader stand together in a kind of acclusion, such that their common knowledge separates them from the remaining characters on the stage."[36] The disciples with others did not grasp the reality as distinct from appearance.

Jesus was clued in. This can be illustrated in various ways, but none more striking than related to His use of the Son of Man designation. Mark records it the first of fourteen times in confirming His authority to forgive sins (2:10). Jesus opted for it again to assert His authority over the Sabbath (2:28), and to refer to His impending death (8:31). Such instances, when taken together, reflect His Messianic awareness.

They also suggest that Jesus wanted the reality to sink in rather than introducing it prematurely.

Where demons were involved, their testimony might have discredited Him. Where those healed were involved, He likely did not want to be known primarily as a wonder-worker or at all as a political or military deliverer. (Where other explanations fail) there is a tension between the known and unknown, between the revealed and the veiled.[37]

The demons were clued in. "I know who you are," an evil spirit cried out, "the Holy One of God" (1:24). "What do you want of me?" asked another, while identifying Jesus as the "Son of the Most High God" (5:7).

The latter instance invites some elaboration. When Jesus got out from the boat, a demoniac came from the tombs to meet Him. "No one was strong enough to subdue him. Night and day among the tombs and in the hills he would cry out and cut himself with stones."

"When he saw Jesus from a distance, he ran and fell on his knees in front of him." Not as a sign of devotion, but recognition of a superior--in contrast to his previous unrestrained behavior. The demon appears as if resigned to its fate, and wishes only to negotiate a settlement.

The audience was clued in. Mark makes a point of doing so at the outset. We are primed to read of the good news about Jesus Christ, the Son of God.

Mark does not allow us to forget what the narrative is all about. He accomplishes this through Jesus' words and works, and the response of others to Him and them. He moves quickly from one instance to the next, so not to lose the trail. He writes as a man with a mission.

As for the disciples, they resembled the blind man of Bethsaida. When Jesus had anointed his eyes, He asked whether the man could see anything (8:23). Looking up, he replied: "I see people; they look like trees walking around."

It was not until Jesus put His hands on the man's eyes a second time that He saw clearly. So it was not until later that the disciples got a firm grasp on reality.

As for the multitudes, they had not experienced the first touch. They remained locked into their blindness.

Appearances

After John was put in prison, Jesus went into Galilee "preaching the good news of God" (1:14). As He was walking by the Sea of Galilee, he called His first disciples--Simon and his brother Andrew (1:16-18). A little further on, He called James and John (1:19-20). After this, He went to Capernaum--located on the northwestern shore of the Sea of Galilee (1:21), and sitting astride the *Via Maris* (Way of the Sea) trade route.

Except for excursions to the "vicinity of Tyre" (7:24), and Caesarea

Philippi (8:27), Jesus seemed content to abide in Galilee. It was at the time spotted with villages, and conducive to the good life. Josephus reported that no part was left uncultivated.

Grapes, pomegranates, olives, and grains grew in abundance. The Sea of Galilee made possible a profitable fishing enterprise.

The inhabitants of Galilee were largely Jewish, and intensely patriotic. There were many Zealots among them. They might be thought of as freedom fighters or trouble makers, depending on one's point of view.

Those of Jerusalem and Judea took a condescending and even contemptuous attitude toward the Galileans. Jerusalem was said to resemble the Holy of Holies, and Galilee the Court of the Gentiles (because of Gentile presence in the area). The Galileans also spoke with a rough dialect, unpleasing to the refined ear of the Judeans.

Jesus was one of them, and recognized as such. So as a rule were His disciples.

Life centered in the family. The rabbis reasoned that three combine in creating life: God, father, and mother. Those who honor father and mother, honor God. If one would benefit from the best of this life and that to come, let him honor his Father in heaven and earthly parents.

Jesus grew up in a village setting. He was a carpenter by trade. "The carpenter measures with a line and makes an outline with a marker; he roughs it with chisels and marks it with compasses" (Isa. 44:13). "With such basic instruments, he fashioned yoke and plow, doors, locks, roofs, windows, low tables, chairs and stool, and storage chests. Most woodwork was rough but some could be ornate--such as lattice work for windows and decoration for the doors."[38]

Family and village life are reflected in the complaint: "Isn't this the carpenter? Isn't this Mary's son and the brother of James, Joseph, Judas and Simon? Aren't his sisters here with us?" (6:3). "They found it difficult to believe he was any better than they or his family were. In their opinion he was nothing more than an ordinary craftsman. Their physical knowledge of Jesus prevented them from having a spiritual knowledge of Him."[39] Appearances deceived them.

"When the Sabbath came, Jesus went into the synagogue and began to teach" (1:21). "Another time he went into the synagogue" (3:1). "When the Sabbath came, he began to teach in the synagogue" (6:2). Luke observes that Jesus "went into the synagogue, *as was his custom*" (4:13).

Synagogue liturgy comprised two primary elements: prayer and the reading of Scripture, to which a homily might be added if a qualified person were available. Jesus was from time to time called upon to read and comment on the Biblical text. As observed by the Jewish writer Samuel Sandmel, He was a "son of the synagogue".

Not to be overlooked, the synagogue was associated with the Pharisaic movement.

> In the one instance recorded in the New Testament in which Jesus argues with the Sadducees--on the question of resurrection--he sides with the Pharisees (see Matt. 22:23). And Jesus' denunciation of war and violence as well as his overall intensification and extension of basic Pharisaic doctrine suggest that, like Paul, he too was nurtured in the Pharisaic camp and considered himself part of it.[40]

If not actually a part, perhaps a close relative.

Relationship aside, the Pharisees generally appear in an adversarial role. They question Jesus' eating with tax collectors and sinners (2:16), and why His disciples do not fast according to their custom (2:18). They complain that the disciples profane the Sabbath (2:24), and fail to follow ritual preparation for eating (7:5). They demand of Jesus a sign to authenticate His ministry (8:11). Jesus denounces them in common with the Herodians (3:6; 8:15).

"Leave them," Jesus urged His disciples, "they are blind guides. If a blind man leads a blind man, both will fall into a pit" (Matt. 5:14). Press toward the light. What you see imperfectly will come into clear focus.

Things came to a head as Jesus and His disciples were traveling through the villages around Caesarea Philippi. The dominant topographical feature in the region is a sheer rock cliff with grotto from which flows one of the tributaries of the Jordan River. Here the god Pan was worshipped.

Religious symbolism abounded. A virtually perpendicular cliff entices one's eyes toward the heavens. The living (running) water speaks of cleansing and renewal. As a religious sanctuary from antiquity, it bore witness to truths obscured by sin. It was likely here that Jesus chose to press the issue.

"Who do people say that I am?" he asked (8:27). Moments later, Jesus wants to know who they think Him to be.

> In the Gospel the term "men" is usually shaded to mean those from whom revelation remains veiled (Chs. 1:17; 7:7f.; 9:31; 10:27; 11:30) as opposed to the disciples who have been extended special grace. The double question of verses 27 and 29 thus permits a sharp differentiation between the inadequate opinions of "men" and the affirmation of faith uttered by

Peter.[41]

With Peter's response, appearance yields to reality.

Reality

Tragedy supposes that a door opens to reality. We must recognize it and enter through it. Jesus as the Christ was such an entrance (8:29). Once Peter had confessed his faith, Jesus began to tell the disciples of His impending death.

Circumstances were for the moment irrelevant. This was the moment of truth. Reality was beckoning.

Reality apprehension "implies a glimpsing of the nature of the UNIFIER or the workings of the universe."[42] The finite plug into the ground of its being. Appearances lose their individual character to form a meaningful whole.

After this, the line between disciple and others will be sharply drawn.

> Tragic man's quest inevitably engages him in a break with those of his fellow men whose concern is mainly for security, in a surrender of his person to the painful experience of fully exercising his freedom, in an act of self-destruction which may end as mere destruction, or as sacrificial immolation, or a new faith.[43]

Except for *mere destruction*, it was all the above from Paul's perspective. "I have been crucified with Christ," he confidently reported, "and I no longer live, but Christ lives in me" (Gal. 2:20). "Therefore, I urge you, brothers, in view of God's mercy, to offer your bodies as living sacrifices, holy and pleasing to God--this is your spiritual act of worship" (Rom. 12:1).

Tragedy coaches us to think in dynamic terms. Not only do we tie into the ground of our being, but the "INEVITABILITY of the universe."[44] We focus on what will eventually come to pass, and press toward that end.

John anticipates as follows: "The throne of God and of the Lamb will be in the city, and his servants will serve him. They will see his face, and his name will be on their foreheads" (Rev. 22:3-4). There will be no more curse, and there will be no more night.

Those so convinced resemble pilgrims traveling to a far country. This world is no longer home. They instead look "forward to the city with foundations, whose architect and builder is God" (Heb. 11:10).

Mark reveals a cosmic struggle of awesome proportions. This is most dramatically illustrated in Jesus' confrontation with the demons. "Have you come to destroy us?" one asked (1:24). It could not imagine a more conciliatory option.

The struggle extends to the religious, social, and political establishment. Thus "the Pharisees went out and began to plot with the Herodians how they might kill Jesus" (3:6).

Jesus engaged in the struggle when He ministered to persons subject to a fallen world. He proclaimed deliverance for those in bondage, and practiced healing of the infirm.

The demands were heavy. From time to time, Jesus retired to some solitary place. Not uncommonly, the multitude followed Him. On one instance, they preceded Him in anticipation of His arrival (6:33). Even in pagan territory, a desperate woman pressed Him with her petition (7:24).

The struggle would not diminish. To the contrary, it would build. There would be wars and rumors of wars. Nation would rise against nation. There would be apostasy and desolation. "If the Lord had not cut short those days, no one would survive" (13:20).

Righteousness will eventually triumph. The present struggle resembles the travail of birth (13:17). After this, the weary world will harvest the *shalom* of God. For now, the disciples experience an earnest of the future.

"Peace I leave with you," Jesus promised; "my peace I give you" (John 14:27). Not as the world gives, only to take it back. "Do not let your hearts be troubled and do not be afraid."

Security-minded persons want no part of the struggle. They drag their feet, hoping to buy more time.

Pressed for a decision, they become more defensive. They have other matters to consider. They must weigh the implications further. Whatever the reason, they refuse to act in faith.

"Who do you say I am?" Jesus insisted. His question was personal and emphatic. Peter's answer was without equivocation: "You are the Christ." Such was reality in crisis perspective.

While the tragedy has reached its crisis, the plot must still run its course. How this reality will impact on the disciples remains to be seen.

One thing was certain from the outset: they will travel a way diverging from the rest. C.S. Lewis referred to this as "the great divorce" . Seemingly small at the time, it broadens out into a deep ravine in eternity.

Mark played to a mixed audience. Some had put their faith in Jesus. For them, there could be no turning back.

Others had not yet responded. The door was ajar for them. They could pass through or turn away. Whatever their decision, God would honor it.

Chapter 6

SUFFERING

Jesus then began to teach His disciples that he would suffer and be killed, and after three days rise from the dead. He spoke plainly, setting parables aside, so that there would be no uncertainty. At this, Peter began to take issue with Him.

The Master, in turn, rebuked His presumptuous disciple. "Get behind me, Satan!" He said (8:33). "You do not have in mind the things of God but the things of men."

Then He summoned the crowed to listen in on His extended comments. "If anyone would come after me, he must deny himself and take up his cross and follow me. For whoever wants to save his life will lose it, but whoever loses his life for me and for the gospel will save it." What good is it to gain the whole world, and forfeit his soul? "Or what can a man give in exchange for his soul?"

"If anyone is ashamed of me and my words in this adulterous and sinful generation, the Son of Man will be ashamed of him when he comes in his father's glory with the holy angels." Tit for tat!

In His Steps

Jesus turned His face resolutely toward Jerusalem. His disciples were to follow in His steps.

It was not a pleasant prospect. Suffering seldom is, and especially when it does not fit with our preconceived ideas--as in this instance.

> (Peter's) response to Jesus' solemn prophecy betrayed no higher level than that characteristic of unregenerate human nature. An inability to accept a

suffering Savior involves the refusal of the will of God, whose sovereign disposition of the problem of sin and human rebellion fails to conform to the niceties of human expectation (cf. Isa. 55:8f).[45]

Jesus makes no attempt to justify God's ways to His disciples. He merely confirms the way of the cross to be God's will.

The disciples were not allowed to select the conditions of their suffering. While it is easier to suffer honorably and to the acclaim of others, they were not assured this would be the case. While it is easier to suffer with others than alone, they were not guaranteed this option. While perhaps easier to accept martyrdom than live as those who have died in Christ, the choice would be made for them.

One thing was not left in doubt. When Christ calls a person, He calls him/her to die. Die to self: self-determination, self-sufficiency, self-glory. Calvary is not an option.

Suffering takes place in three stages: with anticipation, sensation, and reflection. How constructively we deal with pain depends largely on the attitude we bring to it. Once convinced that discipleship involves suffering, it will be easier to bear. Once persuaded that it serves to further the kingdom, it can become the cause of rejoicing.

"Suffering always occurs in a *living context*. The agony is embedded in some project, some hope, some relationship."[46] *This* was project redemption; *this* was in hope of life eternal; *this* was in fellowship with Christ.

Even when it comes to the experience *per se*, we are not strictly passive. "A common misconception is that frequent painful experiences favorably condition or desensitize the individual to pain and that consequently the patient is "used to" pain or less bothered by it. Quite the opposite is true in the majority of patients."[47] They become less capable of managing an unpleasant reality.

The disciples would we hope be among the exception. Their faith might be refined in the furnace of affliction.

After this, they could share their experience with others. Thus Mark writes out of a corporate experience with suffering, as an encouragement to subsequent generations of believers. Written in blood, the legacy would indelibly remain.

Jesus did not speak of suffering alone but as a prelude to resurrection. The point seems missed on the disciples. They could think of nothing but the prospect of suffering.

In another context, Jesus observed that a "woman giving birth to a child has pain because her time has come but when her baby is born she forgets the anguish because of her joy that a child is born into the world. So with you: Now is your time of grief, but I will see you again and you will rejoice, and no one will take away your joy" (John 16:21-22). This is the nature of *suffering hope*.

Even so, the "fight is here and now. Hope should never be the excuse for an escape from the present reality, but an incentive towards a more serious and radical commitment to the transformation of the present."[47] Hope keeps us pressing on in the face of seemingly overwhelming obstacles to do God's work in the world.

Early on, Jesus assured His disciples of God's blessing. "Blessed are those who are persecuted because of righteousness," He confirmed, "for theirs is the kingdom of God" (Matt. 5:10).

While John Wenham explores the positive factors in suffering at some length, we will limit ourselves to those that seem more pertinent for the text before us.[48] First, we note the voluntary context of suffering. "*If* anyone would come after me," Jesus warned, "he must deny himself and take up his cross and follow me."

If not, he can go his way. No constraint is laid on him.

We sense the importance of human freedom in achieving spiritual maturity. It is as we exercise our choices responsibly that we come to realize our human potential. If this involves suffering, we are still the beneficiary.

Second, sin is as a rule linked in some fashion to suffering. As for living in a fallen world, it results from original sin cultivated over the ages. As with willful sin, it reminds us of the wrong we inflict on others and ourselves. As concerns Christ, it bears witness to the vicarious character of His sacrifice.

When something has gone wrong, it is good that suffering alerts us to that fact. Were that not so, we would allow the situation to continue. Warned of the problem, we can take corrective measures.

Third, final retribution or recompense awaits the future. God grants us a brief respite to put our house in order. Wenham comments as follows:

> Character is trained by the deliberate maintenance of a selected objective in spite of the immediate impulses to do otherwise. Delay in the apportionment of rewards and punishments therefore serves a twofold purpose. It allows the sinner a prolonged opportunity for repentance, and it provides the believer with an opportunity for deepening his faith and purifying his motives.[49]

God "is patient with you, not wanting anyone to perish, but everyone to come to repentance" (2 Pet. 3:9). "Let us not become weary in doing good, for at the proper time we will reap a harvest if we do not give up" (Gal. 6:9). With these and other like verses, we can footnote Wenham's observation.

Fourth, evil and good impact on others. Persons allege: "I am only hurting myself." Not so! Our behavior invariably impacts on others.

This may be as the result of something we do, or fail to do. In any case, no person is an island to him/herself. As such, suffering ought to act as a social deterrent to sin.

Fifth, Jesus indicated that the supreme good (salvation) would be achieved through suffering. This being so, we ought never to rule out suffering as if contrary to His will in a fallen world. There is a time to avoid it, and a time to embrace it.

When it comes to suffering, we can approach it with confidence that God means it to realize His purposes. We also can rely on His abounding grace. With such in mind, Paul wrote from prison: "I can do everything through him who gives me strength" (Phil 4:13).

Finally, Jesus provided no detailed outline of the course that each would follow. No two disciples would suffer in precisely the same fashion.

After His resurrection, Jesus warned Peter that the time would come when persons "would lead you where you do not want to go" (John 21:18). Peter, seeing John following them, asked: "Lord, what about him?" "If I want him to remain alive until I return," Jesus replied, "what is that to you? You must follow me."

All things considered, "our present sufferings are not worth comparing with the glory that will be revealed in us" (Rom. 8:18). Even now, "we know that in all things God works for the good of those who love him, who have been called according to his purpose" (v. 28). Such was the perspective Jesus intended to foster concerning suffering for His sake and that of the gospel.

In Community

The disciples were to experience suffering in community. First in anticipation of their experience in Jerusalem; then during the passion; and finally as entrusted with Jesus' mission to the world. For present purposes, we will focus our attention on the first of these: in anticipation of their experience in Jerusalem (9:1-10:52).

More precisely, the disciples' suffering can be shown in three connections: the impending death of Jesus, their call, and experience of community. Jesus' demise would put their life at risk.

Survival is the most basic of human concerns. Jesus stared it down with the comment: "For whoever wants to save his life will lose it, but whoever loses his life for me and for the gospel will save it" (8:35). "This is true, not only finally in the death that all must face, but moment by moment, for such selfish life is no true life, but only animal existence. Life, like sand, trickles between our fingers whether we will or no, and to grasp it more tightly means only that it flows the faster from us."[50]

The reverse is also true. When we open our hands to serve God and others, we gain life. God is no person's debtor.

Theory is one thing; practice another. The disciples would be called upon to put Jesus' teaching to the test. Whatever the cost, they must be prepared to pay it in full.

Even so, physical pain may have been the least of their concerns. This is especially true when we weigh in discipleship.

On one occasion, a would-be disciple assured Jesus: "Teacher, I will follow you wherever you go" (Matt. 8:19). At this Jesus responded: "Foxes have holes and birds of the air have nests, but the Son of Man has no place to lay his head." Security, as commonly understood, must be abandoned.

The disciples were becoming painfully aware of this fact. They were to leave the *friendly* region of Galilee, and make their way through the *foreign* district of Perea. (The latter was the least Jewish of the provinces at the time.) They faced an uncertain fate in Judea.

For the present, they took comfort in being with Jesus. He had never failed them. This consolation would be fleeting. He had warned them of His imminent death. They could not imagine what life would be like without Him. Such uncertainty as they felt then was compounded with the prospect of the future.

On another occasion, Jesus sent forth disciples two by two to the villages He would visit. "Go! I am sending you out like lambs among wolves" (Luke 10:3). "The simile points both to danger and to helplessness. God's servants are always in some sense at the mercy of the world, and in their strength they cannot cope in the situation they found themselves. They must look to God."[51]

From the world, they could anticipate hate. This would result in suffering. From God, they could expect love. This was to be their consolation.

People were bringing their children to Jesus, so that He would pray for them (10:13). Seeing this, His disciples took it upon themselves to rebuke them. Perhaps they felt Jesus had more important things to do.

Jesus was indignant. "Let the little children come to me," He insisted, "for the kingdom of God belongs to such as these." Respect and emulate them. If we disrespect any, we diminish all.

The disciples would have cause to remember this event. They would be mocked as followers of a pretentious rabbi from a village of no repute, since Nazareth was not mentioned in the Old Testament writings. Their lives would be cheap as associates of one executed by the authorities. This too added to their suffering.

If survival is our most basic concern, self-actualization may be thought of as our most climactic and comprehensive.

> It seems that when adults have almost entirely satisfied their basic physiological and social needs, they spontaneously begin to have what (Abraham) Maslow called "peak experiences." These experiences are especially intense moments in which an individual is enveloped by the sensations of ecstasy, wonder, and awe.[52]

Maslow maintained that the final stage of fulfillment involves viewing life as a whole through the particular, and the eternal through the temporal and fleeting.

Thus may we understand Jesus' repeated emphasis on a kingdom perspective. Each event must be considered in the light of the kingdom whole, and time with eternity in view.

As a case in point, a rich young man approached Jesus. "Good teacher," he said, "what must I do to inherit eternal life?" (10:17). "Why do you call me good?" Jesus asked in response. "No one is good--except God alone."

Having gotten the man's attention, Jesus continued. "You know the commandments. Do not murder, do not commit adultery, do not steal, do not give false testimony, do not defraud, honor your father and mother." "Teacher," the man replied with perhaps a sigh of relief, "all these I have kept since I was a boy."

Jesus was taken with the person. "One thing you lack," He added. "Go and sell everything you have and give to the poor, and you will have treasure in heaven. Then come, follow me." The inquirer went away sad, because he had great possessions that he refused to part with. The cost of discipleship proved to be too great.

Suffering, as we have seen, extends from the particular (especially related to Jesus' demise) to the general (discipleship as such). It also results from corporate experience.

Paul put the matter simply: "If one part suffers, every part suffers with it" (1 Cor. 12:26). He allows for no exception.

With community in mind, Jesus encouraged His disciples to pray: "Give *us* today *our* daily bread" (Matt. 6:11). None should have more than enough while others go without.

Similarly, they were to pray: "Forgive us *our* debts, as *we* also have forgiven *our* debtors." Even as their concern was to extend to all, it was in all regards--whether of physical or spiritual nature. If anyone lacks in any connection, all suffer as a result.

Success cannot be measured in individual terms. When Jesus' disciples argued over whom would be greatest in the kingdom, He reminded them the first must be last and servant of all (9:35). They would excel only as individual advancement gave way to corporate interest.

Aristotle observed that "to perceive is to suffer" (*De Anima*). Mark's *crisis* segment provides insight previously lacking. Suffering would follow, as certain as the night follows the day.

Those who would escape suffering flee from life. Those who despair of suffering succumb to circumstances. Those who embrace suffering in hope triumph over obstacles. Jesus would not flee nor would He succumb. In the end, He would triumph; as would those who trusted their lives to His care.

Chapter 7

COURAGE

One gets the impression of Jesus striding determinedly toward Jerusalem, and His disciples strung out behind. From time to time, they confer.

Jesus plays the tragic hero from beginning to last. As such, His "courage in the face of an overpowering challenge is astonishing and praiseworthy and thus wins the sympathy of the audience."[53] Because of Him, life takes on a richer meaning. Because of Him, persons walk a little taller. Because of Him, the way seems open.

Tragic Hero Revisited

Scripture uses *talmao* (courage) in both a positive and negative sense. With positive connotation, Joseph of Arimathea "went boldly to Pilate and asked for Jesus' body" (Mark 15:43). With negative connotation, "from that day on no one dared (had the gall) to ask him any more questions" (Matt. 22:46).

Jesus' courage took on heroic quality. That is, it not only contrasted to evil but transcended the good. We can characterize what this entails, but not exhaust it. The whole remains greater than its parts.

Heroic courage is active, not simply passive. Quintus Horatius Flaccus (Horace) observed that "he who has begun his task has half done it. Have the courage to be wise. Begin!" (*Epistles, 1.2.43*). Jesus began with baptism, resisted the temptations, and pursued His ministry.

Now, His public ministry had nearly run its course. He faced the prospect of death. Undaunted, He continued the initiative in journeying to Jerusalem.

The disciples seem as if dragging their feet. Time and again, Jesus reminds them of His destiny. Each time they are closer to their destination.

Heroic courage focuses on major--not minor--concerns. Mark alerted us to this earlier, since Jesus came preaching the kingdom at hand. All other concerns shrink by comparison.

Would-be disciples offered what seemed to them good reason for postponing their involvement. It was not the convenient time. Other things required their attention.

"Seek first his kingdom and his righteousness," Jesus urged them (Matt. 6:33). Lesser matters will fall into place.

Heroic courage prompts us to look up, not at our feet. Since Jesus insisted on doing good on the Sabbath, He was persecuted (John 5:16). In response, He explained: "My Father is always at his work to this very day, and I, too, am working."

Faced with the cruel prospect of execution, Jesus prayed: "*Abba*, Father, everything is possible for you. Take this cup from me. Yet not what I will, but what you will" (Mark 14:36).

Obstacles appeared as if stepping stones, allowing Him to gain higher ground. Once there, He could continue to climb--as the heavens opened to greet Him.

Heroic courage presses beyond fear, not in its absence. It is human to fear, and Jesus was not immune.

Fear serves a constructive purpose. It alerts us to danger. It cautions us against taking unnecessary risks. It teaches us to be concerned for others.

Paul Tillich suggested that we need to balance fear with courage. Without the former, we lay aside our protective mechanism. Without the latter, we are incapacitated.

Jesus did not need to be reminded of what awaited Him in Jerusalem. A foolish person might not have felt fear, but Jesus was not foolish. He sensed fear and pressed on.

Heroic courage reflects noble qualities, not perverse. "I have shown you many great miracles from the Father," Jesus responded to His accusers. "For which of these do you stone me?" (John 10:32). They did not challenge His doing good, but quickly changed the issue.

Jesus charged that His disciples "let your light shine before men, that they may see your good deeds and praise your Father in heaven" (Matt. 5:16). As was His intent, as He went about preaching the good news and healing.

People for the most part thought of Jesus as a good person. It was hard to find fault with him. Those who did so were themselves less praiseworthy. In thinking to diminish Him, they exposed their frailty.

Heroic courage accepts what can be done, not refrain for lack of a better option. Jesus told a parable concerning the kingdom. "It is like a mustard seed, which is the smallest seed you plant in the ground. Yet when it is planted, it grows and becomes the largest of all garden plants" (Mark 4:30). What may seem of little consequence today, can take on major proportions tomorrow. If, that is, we do not despise a meager start.

"I tell you the truth," Jesus solemnly declared, "anyone who gives you a cup of water in my name because you belong to Christ will certainly not lose his reward" (9:41). It need not be a lavish feast. Whatever we can do, we ought to do.

Jesus seized on the opportunities afforded Him. When rebuffed, He went on to those more receptive. When welcomed, He ministered as allowed. It would appear that He often returned to pick up where He left off, at a more opportune time.

Heroic courage presses resolutely on, not counting the cost. Jesus made this quite clear to His disciples. Those who seek to gain their life will lose it; those willing to surrender their lives for His sake and that of the gospel will save it.

Jesus was given considerable reason to reconsider. The religious establishment was restrained at the outset, and hostile as time passed. The multitude seemed indecisive. The disciples were slow to learn.

"From this time many of his disciples turned back and no longer followed him" (John 6:66). It must have been a discouraging moment. Turning to the twelve, Jesus asked: "You do not want to leave too, do you?" Regardless, you sense that He would have continued without wavering from His course.

Heroic courage reveals grace under pressure, not determination alone. So are we reminded by Jesus frequent recourse to prayer. Revived in spirit, He plunged back into His demanding ministry.

"Why couldn't we drive it (the demon) out?" asked Jesus' disciples (9:28).

> In response to the inevitable question of why they had failed, Jesus explained to the disciples that such malign evil spirits can be expelled only by a full reliance upon the unlimited power of God expressed through prayer. The response contains at less the implicit criticism that the disciples had failed because they had not acted in prayer and sincere faith.[54]

Determination void of grace proved to be deficient.

Jesus succeeded where His disciples had failed. "You deaf and dumb spirit, I command you to come out of him and never enter him again." The spirit shrieked, created violent convulsions, and departed. It had more than met its match.

Heroic courage exhibits freedom, not constraint.

> The end is not known. The limits of human freedom are not known. There is no defining these limits beforehand, because the terms of the definition are themselves indefinite! We speak of human but mean superhuman; we probe godlike freedom without being able to measure what is godlike.[55]

We express such freedom in the use of language, so that man can speak of things removed in space and time. His powers extend to the capacity of storing information for future use. He is freer still, capable of acting on his accumulated knowledge. "He is his own arbiter, mover of himself, a creature loosed into the universe with a power to change it irrevocably."[56]

So it seems in heroic terms. Actually, he squanders his God-given talents. Abusing his freedom, he becomes enslaved.

Mark provides a prime exception, Jesus! He appears in full heroic character as God's Anointed. He is free to serve God, and minister to others.

Heroic courage clothes itself in mystery, not with precision. "If drama in general holds the mirror up to our lives, then tragic drama reflects life's mystery."[57] As Paul put it: "Now we see a poor reflection as in the (burnished) mirror" (1 Cor. 13:12).

We cannot know in any detail what the future holds. When the time comes, what the prophets refer to will be clear.

We cannot even know how our present activity will impact on the future. We trust that God will give us the grace to do what is right, and leave the results in His hands.

We can choose to walk in the light we have. This is the surest way of gaining new insight. It is the heroic thing to do.

The Heroic Few

It seems plausible that Mark meant to represent the disciples with Jesus as a heroic collective. Richard Palmer explains the literary concept:

As long as the stimuli for response presented by pairs of characters maintain an interwoven relationship the audience reacts intensely to both characters (or to a group as a collective protagonist), a tragic response can result. Nothing requires that a single hero embody the source of the tragic experience.[58]

As earlier observed, the *crisis* serves to separate the disciples from the rest. They become the insiders; others remain on the outside. They assume heroic character if only to a modest extent.

Their courage needed to be cultivated. Initially, Peter contested the road to Calvary. As for Jesus' rising from the dead, the disciples discussed among themselves what this might mean (9:10). They did not understand, and were afraid to ask (9:32). "Probably they feared further questioning about what Jesus said due to the apprehension of facing a complete revelation of the suffering that lay ahead."[59]

The transfiguration must have been a confidence builder. Jesus took Peter, James, and John with Him up a high mountain (9:2). There He was transfigured before them. Moses and Elijah appeared with Him, the three talking together.

Fear overcame the disciples. Peter blurted out: "Rabbi, it is good for us to be here. Let us put up three shelters--one for you, one for Moses and one for Elijah." However understood, he put Jesus on a par with the others.

At this, a cloud appeared and engulfed them. A voice spoke from the cloud: "This is my Son, whom I love. Listen to him!" "Suddenly, when they looked around, they no longer saw anyone with them except Jesus."

Jesus instructed them not to speak of what they had seen until after His resurrection. For now, it would serve to bolster their resolution, and indirectly that of the other disciples.

Their confidence was put to the test. Upon coming down the mountain, they found a large crowd surrounding the other disciples, and the teachers of the law arguing with them. "What are you arguing with them about?" Jesus asked (9:16).

Learning that it had to do with the disciples' failure to exorcise a demon, He put the latter to flight. So as to explain their lack of success, Jesus replied: "This kind can come out only by prayer." The text addresses disciples frustrated by spiritual impotence. It reminds them of Jesus authority over the demonic forces. It also encourages them to believe that they can be the channels of God's grace, if they are willing to accept spiritual discipline.

It finally suggests that they emulate the petition of the demoniac's father. "I do believe," he responded to Jesus, "help me overcome my unbelief!" In other words, grant me the courage to believe!

The disciples' fruitless argument over who would be greatest was likely brought on by Jesus taking the three with Him to the mountain top. In this and a future instance, Jesus commented on children concerning discipleship (9:33-37; 10:13-16). He appears to appeal for humility in both instances. As He had earlier taught, "blessed are the poor in spirit, for theirs is the kingdom of heaven" (Matt. 5:3).

No sooner had Jesus said this than He added: "Blessed are those who mourn, for they will be comforted." With these and other words, He meant to strengthen them for the demands ahead.

"Teacher," John spoke, "we saw a man driving out demons in your name and we told him to stop, because he was not one of us" (9:38). "The problem as presented here is not that the man was not following Jesus, but that he was not following the Twelve."[60] It seems to suggest a defensiveness decidedly short on courage.

"Do not stop him," Jesus responded. "No one who does a miracle in my name can in the next moment say anything bad about *me*, for whoever is not against *us* is for *us*." If not contrary to Jesus, it ought not to offend His disciples. Have confidence!

The demands of discipleship are great. "If your hand causes you to sin, cut it off" (9:43). "Therefore what God has joined together, let man not separate" (10:9). "It is easier for a camel to go through the eye of a needle than for a rich man to enter the kingdom of God" (10:25). The disciples were profoundly shaken, and reasoned among themselves: "Who then can be saved?"

Looking at them, Jesus responded: "With man this is impossible, but not with God; all things are possible with God" (10:27). As concerns man, salvation is not simply difficult but impossible. It is instead God's prerogative. Courage needs to draw not from a stagnant puddle, but from living (flowing) water.

They had made their way to Jericho, located about ten miles northwest of the Dead Sea, and fourteen plus miles away from their destination--Jerusalem. As Jesus and His disciples were leaving the city on the last leg of their journey, blind Bartimaeus called out: "Jesus, Son of David, have mercy on me!" (10:47). When some tried to quiet him, he shouted all the more: "Son of David, have mercy on me!"

Jesus stopped and asked that the man be brought to Him. "Cheer up! On your feet! He's calling for you." Hearing this, the man threw off his cloak, jumped to his feet, and came to Jesus. Receiving his sight, he followed Jesus--whether as a disciple or pilgrim we cannot be certain.

Bartimaeus, in contrast to the disciples, was an outsider. He cried out to Jesus in desperation.

He nonetheless exhibited courage. He was anxious to leave the security of blindness for the challenge of sight. As such, he served as a final encouragement to the disciples.

If allowed to turn the pages of history, we read: "When they saw the courage of Peter and John and realized that they were unschooled, ordinary men, they were astonished and they too note that these men had been with Jesus" (Acts 4:13). That is, they recalled that Jesus had displayed similar courage. Jesus and disciples came to be seen as a heroic community.

Mark seems to suggest that this was in the making. The seed of courage was sown; it would bear fruit.

Chapter 8

ORACLES

"The dramatic device called *final oracles* appears in tragedies in which the hero, on the verge of disaster, utters through supernatural insight or out of sheer desperation, oracles announcing the doom of his adversaries."[61] Jesus' announcement that while condemned to death He will be raised from the dead implies retribution, a conclusion emphatically set forth with His discussion of the end times (13:1-37).

For all practical purposes, we have reached the *denouement*. The *crises* is past, as is the *complication*. We anticipate a fallout from what has transpired up to the present, as Mark presses on to his conclusion.

Prophecy in Context

> What do you think about when the subject of prophecy is mentioned? A gypsy fortune teller, bent over her crystal ball, peering into the future? An elaborate wall chart, marked in contrasting colors, detailing events of the last time? These images mislead us into thinking prophecy is primarily concerned with revealing future events.[62]

Prophecy does not serve expressly to reveal the future but disclose God's will. It does not mean to satisfy our curiosity but correct our course.

Jesus' first touches on His death and resurrection (8:31). All else would be extrapolation.

We will look at Jesus' death and resurrection as separate events, then in combination, and finally as they relate to His adversaries. To state the obvious, Jesus' death would be actual. Mark knows nothing of Hugh Schonfield's The Passover Plot.

This was the cause of Peter's concern. He choked on Jesus' words. Pulling Jesus aside, he did his best to dissuade Him.

Jesus' death would also be vicarious. "For even the Son of Man did not come to be served, but to serve, and to give his life as a ransom for many" (10:45). "The ransom metaphor sums up the purpose for which Jesus gave his life and defines the complete expression of his service. The prevailing notion behind the metaphor is that of deliverance by purchase, whether a prisoner of war, a slave, or a forfeited life is the object to be delivered."[63]

Isaiah used a different metaphor for similar intent. "We all, like sheep have gone astray, each of us has turned to his own way; and the Lord has laid on him the iniquity of us all" (Isa. 53:6). Still bent on exploring the theme of vicarious suffering, "for the transgression of my people he was stricken" (v. 8). Still on course, "by his knowledge my righteous servant will justify many" (v. 11). Resolute to the end, "for he bore the sin of many, and made intercession for the transgressors" (v. 12).

Implied as well, Jesus' death would be effective. Where other means had failed, Jesus would succeed.

Albert Sweitzer portrays Jesus as laying hold

> of the wheel of the world to set it moving on that last revolution which is to bring all ordinary history to a close. ...The wheel rolls onward, and the mangled body of the one immeasurably great Man, who was strong enough to think of Himself as the spiritual ruler of mankind and to bend history to His purpose is hanging upon it still. That is His victory and His reign.[64]

Jesus would triumph via death.

His death eventuates in resurrection. Mark describes the women as they wind their way to the tomb to anoint Jesus' body. "Who will roll the stone away from the entrance," they inquire of one another (16:3). But when they look up, they see a young men dressed in white. "Don't be alarmed," he said. "You are looking for Jesus the Nazarene, who was crucified. He is risen!" It was as Jesus had predicted.

Mark, no less than Peter on Pentecost, fearlessly announces Jesus' resurrection. It serves as evidence that the day of deliverance has come. This being so, persons ought to repent of their sin and turn in faith to Christ. Thus they will come to experience resurrection power.

Jesus spoke of His death and resurrection as if prime aspects of one decisive event in history. In greater detail, He alluded to His suffering, rejection, execution, and resurrection (8:31).

"He was delivered over to death for our sins," Paul recalls, "and was raised to life for our justification" (Rom. 4:25). He binds dying and rising together in perhaps a confessional commentary on Isaiah 53:12.

The dynamic relationship of Jesus' death and resurrection may be expressed as *death to life*. They are as the mode of salvation indivisible, and so would be affirmed by succeeding generations.

What Mark implies, Peter spells out in certain terms. "Men of Israel, listen to this: God has made this Jesus, whom you crucified, both Lord and Christ" (Acts 2:36). No wonder they "were cut to the heart," and asked what they could do. They had inadvertently set themselves against God and His anointed. Their doom was sealed unless some solution could be found. This was a matter too urgent to be postponed.

This would become clear in retrospect. As for now, Jesus will take the lead. Others will follow behind Him, astonished at His attitude in anticipation of death, and fearful of what may befall them (cf. 10:32).

Jesus follows His announcement of death-resurrection with a prediction variously understood. "I tell you the truth," He said, "some who are standing here will not taste death before they see the kingdom of God come with power" (9:1). "Those who are standing here" could be a reference to the disciples or the multitude. That some would not taste death seems to imply that some would.

Various commenators suggest that the kingdom coming with power refers to Jesus' transfiguration, six days later. Others prefer the resurrection, Pentecost experience with the Holy Spirit, or *parousia* (*presence, coming*).

Perhaps we would do better to take the prediction in more general terms. In the events soon to follow, the kingdom would be manifest. As the *denouement* unfolds, the disciples would have various occasions to recall Jesus' prophecy and attest its truth.

"As they were on their way up to Jerusalem," Jesus took His disciples aside to emphasize again the purpose of their journey (10:32). On this occasion, Jesus introduces Gentiles as contributing to His suffering. They will mock Him, spit on Him, flog and kill Him.

Jesus may have had in mind Psalm 2. "Why do the nations conspire and the peoples plot in vain? The kings of the earth take their stand and the rulers gather together against the Lord and against his Anointed One" (vv.1-2).

If so, we need to read further. "The One enthroned in heaven laughs; the Lord scoffs at them. Then he rebukes them in his anger and terrifies them in his wrath."

Though the Gentiles rebel, God establishes His kingdom with power. "*I* have installed my King" (v. 6); *I* will proclaim the decree" (v. 7); *I* have become your Father" (v. 7); *I* will make the nations your inheritance (v. 8). "Therefore, you kings, be wise; be warned, you rulers of the earth" (v. 10). Serve the Lord with fear, and embrace the Son lest you anger Him.

Of encouragement to Jesus' disciples, "blessed are all who take refuge in him" (v. 12). They resemble those who find shelter in the cleft of a rock against the storms of life.

As Jesus was leaving the temple, one of His disciples said to Him: "Look, Teacher! What massive stones! What magnificent buildings!" (13:1). "Do you see all these great buildings?" Jesus replied. "Not one stone here will be left on another; every one will be thrown down."

As Jesus was sitting on the Mount of Olives opposite the temple, the inner circle of disciples approached Him. "Tell us, when will these things happen?" they requested. "And what will be the sign that they are all about to be fulfilled?"

Jesus makes no effort to satisfy simple curiosity, but turns to practical concerns. He warns of four dangers: reliance on the outward symbols of faith (v. 2), the deception of Messianic pretenders (vv. 5-6), distraction by world turmoil (vv. 7-8), and being dissuaded by the severity of persecution (vv. 9-13). "To be forewarned, in each case, is to be forearmed. From now on, we move into a climate of increasing violence, and a sense of impending catastrophe."[65]

The disciples' question links the destruction of the temple with the end of the world. Jesus' reply distinguishes between the two. The latter topic begins with "but in those days" (v. 24).

As concerns the destruction of the temple, it resembles the beginning of birth pains (v. 8). Deceivers will multiply; there will be wars and rumors of wars; there will be earthquakes and famines; there will be persecution. "When you see the abomination that causes desolation standing where it does not belong, then let those who are in Judea flee to the mountains" (v. 14).

Initially, the reference was likely to Antiochus profaning the temple with pagan sacrifice. It may have passing application to the presence of Roman standards in the temple precinct, thought to violate the prohibition against idols. Ultimately, it would be embodied in the statue and temple of Zeus built on the temple site after the destruction of 135 A.D.

"But in those days, following the distress," there will be astronomical convulsions, or political upheavals expressed in astronomical terms. "At that time men will see the Son of Man coming in clouds, with great power and glory" (v. 26). He will send His angels and gather the elect from the "four winds".

"No one knows about that day or hour (the end times), not even the angels in heaven, nor the Son but only the Father" (v. 32). This being the case, be on guard. Be alert! "What I say to you, I say to everyone: 'Watch!'" (v. 37).

With this, Jesus draws His disciples' attention back to the turbulent age in which they live. They must be prepared to contend with false teachers, turmoil in society, and persecution. They must respond with vigilant hope.

Vigilant Hope

Mark suggests in broad terms its characteristics. First, it will take the forces of evil seriously. Such as we find illustrated but not exhausted by demonic possession. More subtle but no less a factor, it is expressed by oppressive social, political, and religious institutions.

Daniel Day Williams reasons that the demonic (as representative of evil forces) expresses itself in excitement, distortion, aggrandizement, inertia, and depth of being. "The demonic quickens interest and excitement," he comments. "A dull or boring demon is not worth bothering about."[66]

We are drawn toward evil much as a moth to a light. It holds fascination for us, but turns out to be destructive.

It also distorts our perception of things. Having embraced Satan's lies, we accept them as true.

As Mark casts the role, the deceived remain on the outside. They look on as the *denouement* runs its course. The good news alludes them.

"There cannot be a God, because I could not stand it not to be him," wrote Friedrich Nietzshe. This is the way with aggrandizement. It feeds on domination.

It is diametrically opposed to Jesus' message. "Whoever wants to be great among you must be your servant," He insisted, "and whoever wants to be first must be slave of all" (10:43). So it was with the Son of Man, who came to serve and give His life as a ransom.

Evil opts for the *status quo* in the face of Jesus' call for transformation. It fights to hold back the kingdom of God.

According to Day, this expresses itself not only in oppression but inefficiency. Institutions become bogged down in their bureaucracy, and fail to fulfill their mandate.

Evil erupts with volcanic force from the nature of life as we experience it. It seethes until given opportunity to spread its vile contamination.

Not surprising, those who followed after Jesus felt fear. Jesus was challenging the forces of evil, and all hell might break loose at any moment.

Second, vigilant hope takes the call to discipleship seriously. At Jesus' call to follow Him, James and John left their nets, Simon and Andrew their father, and Levi his custom's booth. In common, they left all.

The rich young ruler was not so disposed. "One thing you lack," Jesus said. "Go, sell everything you have and give to the poor, and you will have treasure in heaven. Then come, follow me" (10:21). "At this the man's face fell. He went away sad, because he had great wealth."

The disciple has to travel light. The way is demanding, and baggage proves burdensome.

On another occasion, Jesus cautioned His disciples against causing any to sin. "It would be better for him to be thrown into the sea with a large millstone tied around his neck," Jesus concluded (9:42). Discipleship must not be weighed lightly.

Third, vigilant hope takes the kingdom leverage seriously. "The kingdom of God provided the necessary purchase for (the disciples, as well as) the prophets. It was their leverage on the most obstinate situation with which they thought to herald the rise and fall of nations and welcome a permanent order. The kingdom was a reality for their time."[67]

As Jesus watched the rich young man retreat into the distance, He exclaimed: "How hard it is to enter the kingdom of God!" (10:23). The disciples were amazed.

"It is easier for a camel to go through the eye of a needle than for a rich man to enter the kingdom of God," Jesus continued. The disciples were even more amazed.

"Who then can be saved?" they asked of one another. None as relates to humans; any as concerns God. "All things are possible with God. Kingdom leverage proves awesome!

Fourth, vigilant hope takes grace seriously. We take grace to mean undeserved favor.

The disciples were not high on the religious pecking order. Others seemed more deserving of God's commendation. In fact, Matthew was a *despicable* tax collector.

Their behavior was periodically subject to criticism. The Pharisees and some of the teachers of the law demanded: "Why don't your disciples live according to the tradition of the elders instead of eating their food with unclean hands?"

No doubt their consciences bothered them from time to time. Having promised to follow Jesus, they kept falling along the way. Guilt tends to crowd out the perception of grace at such times.

Jesus nevertheless taught that they should consider themselves blessed. "Blessed are you when people insult you, persecute you and falsely say all kinds of evil against you because of me," Jesus confided (Matt. 5:11). "Rejoice and be glad, because great is your reward in heaven, for in the same way they persecuted the prophets who were before you."

Reflecting back, Paul observes that "where sin increased, grace increased all the more" (Rom. 5:20). The disciples were recipients of abounding grace.

Finally, vigilant hope takes ultimate victory seriously. *De jure*, the victory has already been accomplished; *de facto*, warfare continues. At times we seem to be making progress, other times the forces of evil rise up as if a raging flood. However uncertain the present may appear, the future stands firm.

This triumphant note washes back into the present. "No (we are not simply sheep for the slaughter), but in all these things we are more than conquerors through him who loved us" (Rom. 8:37). Those who observed Dietrich Bonhoeffer, said of him that he lived as if accustomed to win. Even facing death, he appeared certain and at peace with God.

It could be said of the disciples that they lived their future. They were not so much driven by past experiences as pulled by an irresistible vision of what would be and was becoming.

Chapter 9

FACING UP TO FEAR

According to Aristotle, "the function of tragedy is to arouse in the audience the emotions of fear and pity in order to produce a *catharsis*, or cleansing, of these emotions. The audience feels fear that misfortunes may befall the hero. The audience feels pity because the hero's fortunes gradually decline."[68] If successful, the audience feels purged.

We focus our attention on fear for the present. As a prominent feature of Mark's narrative, it further documents the text as tragedy.

Fears Explored

Mark records fear concerning nature, society, the supernatural, and self. These may appear individually or in some combination.

Concerning nature. Earlier on, we touched on Jesus' stilling the storm (4:39-41). A furious squall came up, and the waves broke over the boat--threatening to swamp it. Jesus was asleep in the stern. The disciples awoke Him with the implied reproach: "Teacher, don't you care if we drown?

Having calmed the wind and waves, Jesus inquired: "Why are you so afraid? Do you still have no faith?"

They continued to be fearful. Terrified, they asked each other: "Who is this? Even the wind and the waves obey him!" They were perhaps more intimidated by their brush with the supernatural than the ominous forces of nature. Even so, the latter provides our immediate concern.

The Sea of Galilee is known for its sudden and turbulent storms. These result from it being in a deep basin surrounded by hills, causing treacherous wind currents. Without warning, nature turns violent.

At such times, a fishing craft is no match for the elements. Nor is the expertise of the fishermen adequate. One cries out for God's intervention, and hopes that his voice is heard above the howling of the wind.

On this occasion, the disciples wondered if Jesus cared that they perish. J. Lincoln Hall generalized this concern with his hymn lyrics: "Does Jesus care when my heart is pained too deeply for mirth and song; as the burdens press, and the cares distress, and the way grows weary and long?"

Unlike the disciples, Hall's faith responded: "O yes, He cares; I know He cares, His heart is touched with my grief; when the days are weary, the long night dreary, I know my Saviour cares." If we understand fear as a question, faith is the answer.

So assured, we turn to another incident. Jairus, one of the synagogue rulers, approached Jesus. "My little daughter is dying," he noted. "Please come and put your hands on her so that she will be healed and live" (5:23). His was the ultimate fear: the prospect of death. "The length of our days is seventy years--or eighty, if we have the strength; yet their span is but trouble and sorrow, for they quickly pass, and we fly away" (Psa. 90:10). As if a whisp of smoke, we fade into oblivion.

While Jesus was still on the way, men came from Jairus' house. "Your daughter is dead," they reported. "Why bother the teacher any more?"

Ignoring what they had said, Jesus encouraged Jairus: "Don't be afraid; just believe." "And so to Jairus as well as to the disciples comes the command to abstain from fear and, instead, *to only believe*."[69]

Jesus continued on to Jairus' house. There was a commotion with people crying and wailing loudly. Upon entering the house, the Master asked them: "Why all this commotion and wailing? The child is not dead but asleep." They laughed at Him.

Putting them with their fear outside, Jesus took Jairus' family and His disciples to the room where the child lay motionless. Ordering her to get up, He took her by the hand. She rose at His command.

Concerning society. Some fears relate to social situations.

> The essential feature of social phobia is a persistent, irrational fear of, and compelling desire to avoid one or more situations in which the individual may be exposed to scrutiny by others. ...Marked anticipatory anxiety occurs if the individual is confronted with the necessity of entering into such a situation, and he or she therefore attempts to avoid it.[70]

An incident is revealing as relates to social phobia. Certain of the religious leaders inquired of Jesus: "By what authority are you doing these things?" (11:28). "I will ask you one question," Jesus replied. "Answer me, and I will tell you by what authority I am doing these things. John's baptism--was it from heaven, or from men? Tell me!"

They reasoned among themselves: "If we say, 'From heaven,' he will ask, 'Then why didn't you believe him?' But if we say, 'From men'... ." They *feared the people*, for they held that John really was a prophet.

As a result, they might lose their leverage with the populace; as a result, their reputation might suffer; as a result, their livelihood might be lost; as a result, their life might be put in jeopardy. No one wanted to risk so much. They answered Jesus: "We don't know."

The disciples were not immune from social phobia. When told that Jesus would be executed, they feared what might happen to them.

Death conceivably was not the worst scenario. Given the disciples' cultural disposition, losing face could be worse. Being cut off from one's people was virtually intolerable. Bringing disgrace on one's family held a horrifying prospect.

Each time fear tugged at their heart strings, they responded with another step toward Jerusalem. So it is with faith, one step at a time. Having decided to follow Jesus, they were determined not to turn back.

Concerning the supernatural. The distinction and relationship between the natural and supernatural differ from culture to culture. What may be thought supernatural in one may be excluded in another. Qualification aside, some distinction and some relationship exist.

With this in mind, we return to the disciples' terrified response: "Who is this? Even the wind and the waves obey him?" (4:41).

> Most personal supernatural powers are involved in making "moral" decisions. That is to say they must decide whether to respond positively or negatively to the request of the suppliant, whose plea is judged as being either ritually or morally justified, or unjustified. Impersonal supernatural powers, however, are usually completely amoral.[71]

The disciples' religious orientation was of a personal (theistic) nature.

Almost without exception, intermediaries assist in communicating with the supernatural. Such appear close to the supernatural, but still able to identify with others. They also serve to shield humans from a direct encounter. The disciples perhaps shared in this perspective.

Mark's short ending also illustrates fear of the supernatural. As mentioned earlier, certain women came to anoint Jesus' body. Arriving at the tomb, they found the stone rolled away. A young man dressed in white robe sat nearby.

"Don't be alarmed," he said. "You are looking for Jesus the Nazarene, who was crucified. He has risen!" (16:6). *Come* see the where He was laid; *go* tell His disciples. "Trembling and bewildered, the women went out and fled from the tomb. They said nothing to anyone, because they were afraid."

Here the preferred text concludes. Not with a resurrection appearance, although this is promised. Not with the women doing as directed, although we learn from other sources that they did so. Not with ecstasy, but fear.

> First, an ending with references to trembling, bewilderment, flight, and fear is not surprising or out of place as many have thought because Mark previously recorded similar reactions when people observed the power of God manifested in Jesus. ...Second, the abrupt ending is quite in harmony with the abrupt beginning of the Gospel. ...Third, Mark had a definite purpose in his ending. ...By stating that the women told no one, he challenged his readers/hearers to assume the responsibility of telling the good news to everyone.[72]

Lastly, all this is consistent with tragic narrative.

Concerning self. "The Son of Man is going to be betrayed into the hands of men," Jesus announced. They will kill him, and after three days he will rise" (9:31). "But the disciples did not understand what he meant, and were afraid to ask him about it."

They may have feared the rebuke of Jesus. Probably they feared a fuller revelation of the suffering that lay ahead, and the burden placed on them to exercise their freedom.

"Moral issues come into being as a consequence of man's freedom, as moral principles come into being as a guide to man in the use of his freedom."[73] Born free, we may act responsibly. Acting responsibly, we make good use of our freedom. Held accountable, we are tempted to flee from freedom.

The scene shifts to Gethsemane. Jesus took Peter, James and John with Him to keep vigil while He prayed. "*Abba*, Father," He said, "everything is possible for you. Take this cup from me. Yet not what I will, but what you will" (14:36). After this, He found the disciples sleeping. Their spirit being willing, their flesh was weak. This scenario played out not once but three times.

Just as Jesus was speaking, Judas arrived to betray Him. He was one of the twelve, but turned Jesus in for thirty pieces of silver.

Peter came to Jesus' defense, striking Malchus--servant of the high priest. "Put your sword back in its place," Jesus ordered him, "for all who draw the sword will die by the sword" (Matt. 26:52). Peter would later deny Jesus.

"Then everyone deserted him and fled" (14:50). "A young man, wearing nothing but a linen garment, was following Jesus. When they seized him, he fled naked, leaving his garment behind." Mark perhaps means to associate his nakedness with the shame borne by the disciples for forsaking Jesus.

Would any of us have done better? No one can say for sure. We hope for the best, but fear for the worst.

Coping With Fear

S.R. Rachman discusses three approaches to reducing fear: *systematic desensitization, flooding,* and *modeling.* While not necessarily exhaustive, they provide interesting insights into Jesus' ministry to the fearful.

First, *systematic desensitization* exposes persons to fear, which in turn may reduce the fear response.

> The complexity of the relations between the emergence and the decline of a fear can be seen from the fact that repeated exposures to the fear-evoking object or situation increase the fear (sensitization) at some times, and at other times decrease it (habituation). ...The balance tilts in the direction of increased or decreased fear depending on the type of exposure, the intensity of the stimulation, the person's state of alertness, and other factors.[74]

Jesus pushed the fear button with His call to discipleship. He invited folk to forsake all to follow Him. As a rule, He did not get down to specifics.

Later on, Jesus reminded His followers of the cost of discipleship. As when He instructed the rich young man to sell everything and give to the poor, and come follow Him.

In the same context, Jesus accented the promise of discipleship. "I tell you the truth," He responded to Peter's comment that they had left all, "no one who has left home or brothers or sisters or mother or father or children or fields for me and the gospel will fail to receive a hundred times as much in this present age, and in the age to come, eternal life" (10:29-30).

The disciples did not key into Jesus' teaching all at once, though a major breakthrough occurred with Peter's confession. Jesus orchestrated their sensitivity training with care, considering the circumstances pressing in on them and the disciples' awareness.

Second, *flooding* involves stepping up the experience of pain. This can be done by way of experience or in anticipation. Either way, it helps us manage fear constructively.

Jesus could have told His flock to stay securely within the pen. Instead, He said to the seventy-two: "Go! I am sending you out like lambs among wolves" (Luke 10:3). "The simile points both to danger and to helplessness. God's servants are always in some sense at the mercy of the world, and in their own strength they cannot cope with the situation in which they find themselves."[75] This could be considered an instance of *flooding*.

Jesus also warned them time and again of what awaited Him in Jerusalem. The prospect for Him and them was ominous. This, too, could qualify as *flooding*.

Third, *modeling* suggests that persons learn by observing others. It was as the disciples observed how Jesus responded to fear that they learned how to do so.

Oscar Cullmann, in a classic passage, contrasted Socrates' approach to death to that of Jesus. "The death of Socrates is a beautiful death. Nothing is seen here of death's terror. ...And now let us hear how Jesus dies. ...Jesus is afraid, though not as a coward would be of the men who will kill him, still less of the pain and grief which precede death itself."[76]

Jesus looked long and hard at the face of death, our final enemy. He lifted His hands in prayer, as He has done at every decisive moment. He was confident.

At the sixth hour, darkness shrouded the scene. At the ninth hour, Jesus cried out: "My God, my God, why have you forsaken me?" (15:34). The words derive from Psalm 22. It was not a lapse of faith, but faith-posturing as death drew near. Not to be overlooked, the psalm anticipates vindication. "I will declare your name to my brothers; in the congregation I will praise you. ...For he has not despised or disdained the suffering of the afflicted one; he has not hidden his face from him but has listened to his cry for help" (22:22,24).

"A useful psychology of death would also be a psychology of life."[77] Conversely, one who is not prepared to die is not prepared to live. Jesus ministered by modeling.

Was Jesus simply making use of dynamics available to others? Likely not! Mark leaves us with the impression that, similarities aside, Jesus was

unique.
C.G. Montefiore would bear this out.

> The methods which Jesus sometimes adopted for the cure of sin were original and startling. It does not follow that in a lesser man these methods would be either justified or successful. It is not every one who can imitate Jesus, and without harm to himself and with benefit to his companions become the friend of sinners.[78]

Jesus was one of a kind.

Mark's characters are real, and their fears real. We can readily identify with them.

Walking on ahead of His disciples, Jesus faces fear valiantly. Looking over His shoulder, we take courage to press on. As He reminds us, "all things are possible with God" (10:27).

Chapter 10

EXPERIENCING PITY

Aristotle coupled fear and pity together in tragic tension. As fear drives us away, so pity entices us to come closer. Tragedy thus "brings the emotions of pity and fear under control by stimulating them to such an immoderate degree that they return to their proper balance in the spectator's emotion makeup."[79]

Pity is a feeling of sympathy and compassion for others in their suffering. It may also be used in contempt, but not in the Biblical setting.

Pathos in Jesus

Pathos refers to the quality that elicits pity. We shall consider the pathos of Jesus from the human, moral, ethnic, and religious perspectives.

The human factor. Jesus was no phantasm but human. We first discover Him requesting baptism. Following this, He walks away into the wilderness to be tested. He is soon vigorously engaged in public ministry. He dies as must we all.

One incident especially comes to mind. When Jesus saw the disciples straining at the oars, because the wind was against them, He came walking on the water. Seeing Him, they were terrified, supposing that He were a spirit (6:49).

At this, Jesus corrected their delusion. "Take courage!" He admonished them. "It is I. Don't be afraid." Then He climbed into the boat, and the wind died down. The disciples marvelled at what sort of person could exercise such authority. If not a water spirit, what then?

Jesus was one human among others.

All the characters who encounter Jesus bear the stamp of this world: the priest and the scribe, the Pharisee and the publican, the rich and the poor, the healthy and the sick, the righteous and the sinner. They appear in the story in a matter-of-fact fashion, chosen at random and of great variety, and appearing in no particular order. Yet all the characters, however great their diversity, present a very human appearance.[80]

While one among others, Jesus was strikingly different. For one thing, He lived out His life in uncorrupted fashion. We see in Him what life would be except for sin, and subsequent to the fall. If anything, He was more human than the rest.

Anything that we may wish to add concerning His deity, does not detract from His humanity. His humanity was not watered down in the incarnation.

This, then, is a major reason for our attraction to Jesus. He is one of us. He faced problems similar to those we face. He felt as we feel. He thought as we think. He acted as must we.

He had to contend with ambiguity. As did Job, when confronted with the simplistic solutions of his accusers. As must we, if candid. Jesus appeals to us as a real person in the real world.

The moral factor. Jesus was a good person. This was evidenced by the good works He did. "A good tree cannot bear bad fruit, and a bad tree cannot bear good fruit. ...Thus, by their fruit you will recognize them" (Matt. 7:18,20).

"Which is lawful on the Sabbath," He asked, "to do good works or evil, to save life or to kill?" (3:4). Taken by itself, the first question begs the question, "since keeping the sabbath law was the "good," unless a greater "good" called for actions that otherwise would have desecrated the sabbath. The real question then becomes, what standard determines the greater good that would permit one to transgress the sabbath?"[81] Jesus suggests the criteria by His second question, "to save life or to kill?".

"Good teacher," the rich young ruler addressed Jesus (10:17). "Why do you call me good?" Jesus answered. While the address was perhaps little more than a compliment, it was not off the mark. Jesus insisted that the man take the implications seriously.

At Jesus' death, the centurion in charge cried out: "Surely this man was the Son of God" (15:39). His meaning is debated. Some think that he intended only to point out Jesus' pious character. Others suppose that he had deeper insight. All would agree that it served Mark's fondness for irony.

Pity thrives on goodness. When one gets what we think they deserve, we show them little pity. Where goodness increases, pity keeps pace.

Jesus was crucified with thieves (15:27). Portrayed as guilty by association, we feel pity for Jesus. Those who passed by hurled insults at Him (22:9). Our pity intensified. The religious leaders mocked Him (22:31). We feel indignation coupled with pity.

Aristotle defined pity as "a sense of pain at what we take to be an evil of a destructive or painful kind, which befalls one who does not deserve it, which we think of ourselves or someone allied to us might likewise suffer, and when this possibility seems near at hand " (*The Rhetoric*, Book 2,5,1). Jesus as a moral paradigm would solicit no less.

The ethnic factor. Jesus was Jewish. "The Hebrew's sense of peoplehood came of age with the exodus. They had resisted the appeal to assimilate in more favorable times, and were drawn together by subsequent oppression. They cried out to the God of their fathers, and He heard their petition--sending Moses to deliver them."[82] Jesus was from this lineage.

Enslavement was past; the promised land lay in the future. God covenanted with His people at Sinai. He would be their God, and they His people. Jesus enjoyed this heritage.

They managed a precarious existence in a buffer zone between two great population centers of antiquity. Their fortunes waxed and waned. They were taken into captivity. Jesus was aware of the problems this created.

They were by Jesus' time subject to Rome. The Jewish response to Hellenism generated various sects. Jesus debated in this sectarian context.

Judaism played to mixed Gentile reviews. On the one hand, its moral rectitude appealed to many; on the other, it seemed unnecessarily rigorous. On the one hand, devotion to the living God seemed more credible than to the Olympic pantheon; on the other, it seemed strikingly intolerant.

A curious reversal took place as the church became increasingly Gentile in orientation. Where once Jesus invoked pity from Jewish believers for His ethnic character, this became decreasingly so. Where once pity was reserved because of His ethnic identity, this became less so.

So far as cultural diversity is prized, Jesus' ethnicity heightens our feeling of pity. We cherish His cultural distinctive, and acutely feel the pain of His undeserved suffering.

The religious factor. Jesus told a parable about a man who planted a vineyard. "He put a wall around it, dug a pit for the winepress and built a watchtower. Then he rented the vineyard to some farmers and went away on a journey" (12:1).

At harvest time, he sent a servant to collect from the tenants what was due him. They seized and beat him, sending him away empty-handed. He sent another servant; they struck him and treated him shamefully. He sent many others; they beat some and killed the remainder.

"He had one left to send, a son, whom he loved." He sent him last, supposing that they would respect him. "This is the heir," they reasoned. "Come, let's kill him, and the inheritance will be ours." So they took and killed him, and threw his body out of the vineyard.

Those implicated understood full well. "They knew he had spoken the parable against them. But they were afraid of the crowd; so they left him and went away."

Those intent on Mark's tragic narrative, feel pity as never before. If to suffer for good encourages pity, then to suffer for God even more so.

Reality replaces parable at Gethsemane. "Take this cup from me," Jesus pleads. "Yet not what I will, but what you will" (14:36). "The last statement is the most important because by it Mark indicates that in the end Jesus was submissive to God's will. His prayer to be spared death was answered in accordance with the divine will. God gave him something better, victory over death."[83]

Death is never far from those we love, nor we ourselves. "The sting of death is sin," Paul observes. "But thanks be to God! He gives us the victory through our lord Jesus Christ" (1 Cor. 15:56-57). When pity has drawn us to the foot of the cross, faith can take over.

Nearer Still

Tragedy also seeks to get us in touch with ourselves. It leads us to consider ourselves in relationship with others.

Mark approaches this task via our association with nature, society, self, and cosmos (with regard to the all-embracing reality). He portrays man as steward of creation. The parable of the tenants, elaborated earlier, illustrates this fact (12:1-12). We, like the tenants in the parable, are to cultivate God's vineyard. He will hold us accountable.

Previously, Jesus told the parable of a sower (4:1-20). "Listen!" He said. "A farmer went out to sow his seed." Some fell along the path, on rocky ground, or among thorns--with poor results. "Still other seed fell on good soil. They came up, grew and produced a crop, multiplying thirty, sixty, or even a hundred times."

He said this to account for the various responses to the gospel concerning the kingdom. In more subtle fashion, it illustrated our stewardship relationship to creation.

As observed in another context, nature from time to time turns chaotic. As when a furious squall came up, it threatened to swamp the boat (4:37). At such times, the steward turns survivor. Thus when an adversarial wind persists, the disciples strain at their oars to reach safety (6:48).

"Everyone who hears these words of mine and puts them into practice," Jesus observed, "is like a wise man who built his house on the rock" (Matt. 7:24). The rains come, the streams rise, and the wind blows and beats against the house; but the house withstands the test.

"But everyone who hears these words of mine and does not put them into practice is like a foolish man who built his house on sand." When the rain comes, the streams rise, and the wind blows and beats against his house, it collapses with a deafening sound. As we prepare for chaotic times, so we fare during them.

We also are involved in a multi-faceted social matrix. Mark introduces the family as of prime importance. We read that when Jesus' family heard of the astonishing results of His ministry, they thought Him out of His mind (3:21). Assuming their filial responsibility, they set out to take Him into custody.

"Standing outside, they sent someone in to call him" (3:31). "'Standing outside' appears to offer an important contrast to those 'seated around him' somewhat in keeping with 4:10-11. Certainly, the contrast becomes clear in the comments that follow between the 'mother and brothers' outside and the 'mother and brothers' around Jesus inside."[84]

Who are my mother and my brothers?" Jesus responded. Looking around at those seated in a circle around Him, He said: "Here are my mother and my brothers! Whoever does God's will is my brother and sister and mother." He said this not to repudiate the natural relationship, but emphasize the spiritual.

Jesus reaffirmed the family relationship from the cross. When Jesus saw His mother and beloved disciple standing near, He said to her: "Dear woman, here is your son," and to him: "Here is your mother" (John 19:26). "From that time on, this disciple took her into his home."

Jesus legitimized other than family relationships. These extended throughout society: concerning male and female, also adult and youth, among peers, with vocational pursuits, with the rights of passage, among others.

One illustration will suffice. A leper came to Jesus with petition implied: "If you are willing, you can make me clean" (1:40). Moved with compassion, Jesus reached out His hand and touched the man. "I am willing," He said. "Be clean!" Immediately he was cured.

"See that you don't tell this to anyone," Jesus added. "But go, show yourself to the priest and offer the sacrifices Moses commanded for your cleansing, as a testimony to them." It was the priest's responsibility to declare him clean, and countenance his return to normal social relationships.

Mark also testifies to the importance of introspection. "Listen to me, everyone, and understand this," Jesus solemnly announced. "Nothing outside a man can make him 'unclean' by going into him. Rather, it is what comes out of a man that makes him 'unclean'" (7:15). Look within to discover whether righteous or not.

"Who do people say that I am?" Jesus asked (8:27). His disciples replied: "Some say John the Baptist; others say Elijah; and still others, one of the prophets." Not content, Jesus pressed them further: "But what about you?" Look within for an answer, and key to your identity as disciples.

Introspection nonetheless could lead them astray. "What were you arguing about on the road?" Jesus asked (9:33). The disciples refused to answer, because they had been arguing over whom would be greatest in the kingdom.

Jesus stood a little child among them. Then, taking the child in His arms, Jesus said to them: "Whoever welcomes one of these little children in my name welcomes me, and whoever welcomes me does not welcome me but the one who sent me." That is, consider again!

Finally, Mark stresses our relationship to cosmic reality, expressed in terms of the kingdom of God. "The time has come," Jesus said. "The kingdom of God is near. Repent and believe the good news!" (1:15).

His message never changed or lost its urgency. This is what the kingdom of God is like: "A man scatters seed on the ground" (4:26). The seed sprouts and grows. All by itself the soil produces grain--first the stalk, then the head, then the full kernel in the head. As soon as the grain is ripe, he puts the sickle to it, because it is harvest time.

Again He asked what the kingdom of God was like, "or what parable shall we use to describe it?" (4:30). It is like a mustard seed, small at first and then with lavish growth.

As noted previously, when facing execution, Jesus prayed: "Take this cup from me. Yet not my will, but what you will" (14:36). The kingdom took priority over all other concerns.

Pity cultivates our sensitivity to others and awareness of self. Without it, life becomes little more than the survival of the fittest. With it, life resembles family.

Chapter 11

CATHARSIS

As previously stated, the interaction of fear and pity generates catharsis. Tragedy arouses them so that they are purged, balanced, eliminated, or sublimated in the audience. The explanation varies from one commentator to the next.

With catharsis, we increasingly come to focus on the audience: what it brings to the text, and what it hopes to gain from it. "Tragedy thus stirs within us *what is already there*, what we bring to it as thinking, feeling mortals. It allows us to come to terms with what we know, and it makes us realize that we can live with the question mark."[85]

The Already There

"Mark probably wrote for a Roman reading audience. He translated Aramaic expressions for the benefit of his readers (3:17; 5:41; 7:34; 14:36; 15:34). Even more indicatively, he explained Greek expressions by their Latin equivalents (12:42; 15:16) and used a number of other Latin terms."[86] He also refers to Rufus (15:21), who according to Romans 16:13 lived in Rome (unless two bear the same name). In addition, 1 Pet. 5:13 locates Mark in Rome (Babylon), as does early Christian tradition.

Mark perhaps wrote during the reign of Nero, 54-68 A.D. The latter was by disposition more an artist than executive. Through carelessness and extravagance, he emptied the public treasury. Attempting to recover, he turned to oppression and violence.

In A.D. 64 a great fire broke out in Rome, destroying a large part of the city. Nero was suspected of having deliberately set the fire in order to make room for the palace he meant to erect on the Esquiline Hill. He accused the Christians to divert blame from himself. Their deliberate separation from pagan practice and talk of the world being destroyed by fire lent credibility to his charge.

Tacitus describes what resulted:

> Those who confessed were first seized, then on their information a great multitude were convicted, not so much of the crime of incendiarism, as of hatred of the human race. The victims who perished also suffered insults, for some were covered with the skins of wild beasts and torn to pieces by dogs, while others were fixed to crosses and burned to light the night when daylight had failed (*Annales, XV,44*).

Tacitus adds this comment: "Although they were criminals who deserved the most severe punishment, yet a feeling of pity arose since they were put to death not for the public good but to satisfy the rage of an individual."

Such were the perilous times in which Christians lived. With this in mind, Mark would have taken pen in hand.

The events that Mark describes had long since passed. As had many interim developments, not least of which was the rapid expansion of Christianity beyond its Jewish confines.

Mark did not have to remind his audience of recent events. Once thought a harmless Jewish sect, the Christian community had become a plausible threat to the *Pax Romana*. Once few, it continued to grow at an *alarming* rate.

Misunderstandings abounded. Some took the Christians' rejection of the pagan gods to mean that they were irreligious and immoral. There were also reports of incest and cannibalism as distortions of fellowship and communion. The Christians hatred of sin was taken to be hatred of humanity.

Mark turned back the pages of history to Jesus. The latter had gone about preaching God's good news, healing the sick, and mending relationships. He persevered even in the face of death. Although executed, God showed His approval of Jesus via the resurrection.

Jesus' disciples could expect no easier a lot in life. They were to serve without thought of recompense. They were to return good for evil. They were to hold fast to their faith despite the cost.

"The consequences of the persecutions are difficult to assess. Rather than stopping the growth of Christianity, they advertised and enhanced its appeal. People dared to be heroic."[87] They triumphed over tradedy.

As representative, the courageous Polycarp stood firm: "Thou threatenest me with fire which burneth for an hour, and after a little is extinguished, but art ignorant of the fire of the coming judgment and of eternal punishment, reserved for the ungodly. But why tarriest thou? Bring forth what thou wilt" (*The Martyrdom of Polycarp, XI*).

Tragedy cultivates such resolve. It "usually steals some victory from death, depriving it of some, but not all, of its pain; approaching it as a new challenge, or, at worst, as a deserved rest from an even more fearful life."[88]

Transitory pain appeared to the early Christians as preferable to everlasting torment. They chose to weigh life in terms of eternity. Mark and Polycarp heartily agreed on this point, and it impacted on all else.

Nero serves as contrast. He indulged himself with all that this world has to offer. Far from satisfied, he feared that others would take his life. If so, all would be lost. When gone, he would be remembered not for his rectitude but rage.

Mark anticipates that there is a potential Nero and Polycarp in each of us. That is what we bring to our reading of the text. How we respond will determine which prevails.

The Not as Yet

Born as the result of physical processes, humans survive through social means. Most critical of these is the family.

"Family in its Latin sense, *familia*, covered every member of the household subject to the powers of the father of the family, the *paterfamilias*."[89] It would involve spouse, children, slaves, and sometimes business associates.

The *paterfamilias'* will was law. For instance, he would arrange marriages as it pleased him. Advancement of family interests took precedence over the desires of the couple. As a result, the Roman household was reported as a hotbed of sexual activity--except between married couples.

The remaining family members were to obey, and so preserve the fragile social structure. Failing to do so, life would come unraveled.

The system could prove a blessing or a curse. One hoped for the best and feared for the worse.

A Roman audience would have listened in on on Jesus' interchange with His family with special interest (cf. 8:20-35). "Mark frequently inserts an event or narrative between two phases of some action of Jesus. This literary device is effective for indicating a lapse of time, for dramatically heightening the tension, or for drawing attention to a significant parallel or contrast."⁹⁰ Here we have the first instance, with the family narrative divided by controversy over Beelzebub.

Mark means to suggest that the concern of Jesus' family was not unlike that of the charge of the scribes. The former concluded that "He is out of his mind" (v. 21), and the latter that "He has an unclean spirit" (v. 30). While distinct from one another, both would restrain Jesus from continuing His work.

Both alike also stand in opposition to those gathered around Jesus. "Here (in contrast to being outside) are my mother and my brothers!" Jesus concluded. "Whoever does God's will is my brother and sister and mother" (vv. 34-35).

One can imagine a sigh of relief from Mark's audience. They have faced the possibility that in following Jesus they will fall out of step with family. As threatening as the prospect might appear, they could by God's grace press on with fear constrained.

The Roman youth had among his earliest memories that of the family's patron deity.

> Philosophers were few, even among the educated, and despite their writings "superstition" was not confined to the lower classes. ..."Atheists" were either Epicureans who denied the gods' providence, but not their existence, or Jews and Christians who worshipped their own God, while denying everyone else's.[91]

The Romans looked back upon a history thought to result from the intervention of their gods.

> This history, as it unfolded in space and time, was the realization of a divinely preordained plan. Roman religion placed heavy emphasis on learning the divine will and assisting the divine fatum toward its process of fulfillment. In this way a harmonious relationship could be maintained between the divine and human spheres; new and unproven religious practices, on the other hand could only disturb this harmony and thus endanger the security of the state.[92]

Christianity appeared as if new and threatening. It might undermine all that had proven worthy of emulation. One's worst fears might be realized.

Mark assures his audience concerning the prophets, a tradition earlier than that of Rome itself. "I will send my messenger ahead of you, who will prepare your way--a voice of one calling in the desert, 'Prepare the way for the Lord, make straight paths for him'" (1:2-3).

While recent in time, the gospel fulfills that promised from antiquity. Now that the time was right, God brought to pass what He had promised.

History would be rewritten around the coming of Christ. "In the past God overlooked such ignorance (as reflected in pagan religious practice)," Paul concluded, "but now he commands all people everywhere to repent" (Acts 17:30).

Not all would embrace Mark's appeal. As in Athens, some would mock, others consider further, and still others believe. If not the best of prospects, then it is not the worst. The Roman convert's fear thus was reigned in.

As for the religious establishment, one might expect the worst. Time and again it had opposed Jesus to protect its self interest. In the end, it engineered His death.

Moved by pity and fear, Mark's audience made its way with Jesus toward Calvary. "Then they offered him wine mixed with myrrh, but he did not take it" (15:23). It was according to Jewish custom to offer a narcotic drink to ease pain (*Sanhedrin 43a*), but Jesus refused it. Perhaps He determined not to take an easier way out than that offered to others; perhaps He meant to stay alert to potential ministry. Whatever the case, He entered fully into human suffering, and to bring healing.

Then "they crucified him." The text says little but evokes much.

> For Constantine, the Crusaders, and for nineteenth-century missions, the cross was a symbol of victory, and expression of the triumph of the gospel. ...For medieval saints and mystics, for modern romantics and pietists, and for simple Christians in every age, Jesus on his cross was and is an object of personal devotion, a call to repentance, an incentive to good works. ...For the poor and oppressed through history, the crucifixion is Jesus' identification in the flesh with the wretched of the earth.[93]

For the Roman convert, it initiated catharsis.

Not to be overlooked, Aelius Aristedes of Smyrna, writing a century later, commented on the *pax Romana*:

> A man simply travels from one country to another as though it were his native land. We are no longer frightened by the Cilician pass or by the narrow sandy tracks that lead from Arabia into Egypt. We are not dismayed by the height of mountains, or by the vast breadth of rivers or by inhospitable tribes of barbarians. To be a Roman citizen, nay even one of your subjects is a sufficient guarantee of personal safely (*Oratio*

XXVI.70&100).

It provided not only freedom of movement, but peace and justice where previously it was lacking.

The cities of the Empire were governed by men who believed in defending Roman order (including religious order) against all that would threaten. Thus the Ephesian city clerk quieted the multitude with the warning: "As it is, we are in danger of being charged with rioting because of today's events. In that case we would not be able to account for the commotion, since there is no reason for it" (Acts 19:40). With this, he dismissed the assembly.

> On the huge capitals of the columns (in Carthage), the emperor himself is shown as Zeus destroying the titans, represented by snake-headed monsters. The provincials were expected to see him as their protector against evil and the forces of chaos that always threatened their existence.[94]

Within there was peace; without there was chaos.

It was a part truth at best. Rome emphatically was not without its faults. Taxation weighed heavily on the populace. Privilege abounded in almost every connection. Responsibility waned in the process. People despaired.

Mark picks up on the peace motif with Christ. Peace not as Rome gives, superficial and fleeting. Peace as Jesus bestows, deeply engrained and constant.

Mark elaborates in at least four connections: with forgiveness, physical needs, meaningful relationships, and self-actualization. As previously noted, Jesus pronounced forgiveness when asked to heal (2:5). Why did Jesus speak in this fashion? Why introduce sin and forgiveness? Had He failed to recognize the man's real need? Yes, He recognized the man's physical need and more. He hoped to minister to the whole person.

Of similar intent, Mark suggests that after Jesus healed a blind man, the latter "followed Jesus along the road" (10:2). Perhaps it was as a disciple or as a literary device to imply discipleship, but in any case with forgiveness-discipleship in view.

Jesus' invitation to follow Him was calculated to increase anxiety over daily sustenance. Jesus invited Simon and Andrew to leave their *nets* (1:18), James and John their *father with hired men and boat* (1:20), Levi his *collector's booth* (2:14), and the young man his *great wealth* (10:21).

Stripped of their means, they faced the prospect of privation.

Jesus elsewhere observed: "Look at the birds of the air; they do not sow or reap or store away in barns, and yet your heavenly Father feeds them" (Matt. 6:26). Look at the birds of the air. If God clothes these, will He not take more care of you?

The point is implicit to Mark's narrative. Those who trust their way to Christ find that they lack nothing. This is graphically illustrated in the feeding of the multitudes (6:30-44; 8:1-13). In each instance, the people were without adequate means (6:38; 8:5). In each instance, Jesus gave thanks for God's provision (6:41; 8:7). In each instance, they had more than enough (6:42-43; 8:8).

The Roman convert also might fear his relationships would be strained. He was fortunate not to have them summarily severed. After all, Christianity was viewed by most as an obnoxious faith and a contagious disease.

Mark touched on this concern in two ways: with the experience of fellowship as such and a life of shared service. As to the former, we discover others through Christ. We are discipled together.

The potential of such relationships is greater for being in Christ. He mediates among us, accenting the good and minimizing the adverse. This brings an exciting new dimension to life together.

We also forge relationships through service. Calling the twelve to Him, Jesus sent them forth two by two to minister (6:7). They went as directed and shared in the joys of fruitful labor.

They were also bonded to those they served. Thus Paul wrote: "I thank God every time I remember you. In all my prayers for all of you, I always pray with joy because of your partnership in the gospel from the first day until now" (Phil. 1:3-5).

Mark finally alludes to self-actualization. As a last resort, the Roman was said to turn "to warfare for self-fulfillment."[95] There was always need for soldiers to serve throughout the far reaches of the Roman Empire. In this capacity, if no other, one might sense fulfillment.

With such in mind, we turn to the anonymous centurian attending Jesus' crucifixion. When at last Jesus breathed His last, the Roman cried out: "Surely this man was the Son of God!" (15:39). What he actually understood remains uncertain. What his statement came to represent is not. As Mark treats the matter, it becomes a confession of faith.

As a Jew, Peter recognized Jesus as the Christ (8:29); now a Gentile soldier recognizes Him as the Son of God. They resemble two peaks rising above a mountain range. They invite us to experience the *pax*

Christos.

After a cathartic encounter with Christ, what then? "Tomorrow is something of a rumor and something of a ruse. Tomorrow is a cleaver and effective way to keep us going. Tomorrow is a point of focus for thoughts and feelings that might otherwise skirl about aimlessly. For myself, I approve of tomorrow, but I don't much trust it."[96] So much for conventional thinking, then and now.

"Therefore do not worry about tomorrow, for tomorrow will worry about itself" Jesus counseled. "Each day has enough trouble of its own" (Matt. 6:34).

With like result, focus on current things in the light of their eventual outcome (13:1-37). Turn your attention to immediate concerns with confidence knowing that *all* things work together for good for those who love God and seek His pleasure.

All it takes is one step at a time. God will take care of the rest. So the Christian thinks, but more of this momentarily.

Chapter 12

BOTTOM LINE

The legacy of tragedy has been variously described. Aristotle observed that it leaves its audience not depressed, but relieved or even exalted. Others point out that it involves the affirmation of life. Still others have alluded to its accent on freedom and consequent responsibility.

As if to sum up: "Tragedy is a terrain, vast, unmapped in advance, waiting for the impress of feet which will not break stride until the last possible step has been taken."[97] We affirm life as an opportunity to serve some noble purpose, ill-defined as it may appear. We press relentlessly toward a distant horizon, not content to linger along the way.

Jesus Christ Superstar

> We have in the synoptic gospels three portraits of Jesus of Nazareth, which although differing in many details, are all concerned with the same person. It is only Mark, of the three, who in the opening words gives an indication that he is introducing more than a man, and yet he, more than the others, concentrates on the human Jesus.[98]

Whatever we can say of others, Jesus supersedes them in every way that genuinely matters. Mark identifies Him as the Christ, the Son of God (1:1).

From this point on, he stresses Jesus' humanity, as if to affirm life in every respect but sin. At John the Baptist's cue, Jesus takes center stage. All else from this moment on revolves around Him. (What follows repeats some things, adds others, accents still others, and summarizes in the process.)

Jesus affirms life in an alienated world. No sooner had He been baptized than the Spirit sent Him into the wilderness to be tempted by Satan (1:12-13). No sooner was He finished teaching than a demoniac insisted on knowing His intention (1:24). No sooner had He pronounced a man's sins forgiven than He was accused of blasphemy (2:7).

With the passing of time, opposition built. When teachers of the law arrived from Jerusalem, they accused Jesus of being possessed by Beelzebub (3:22). When Jesus had returned to Nazareth, the people took offense with Him (6:1). The Pharisees and teachers of the law criticized Jesus' disciples for not abiding by the tradition of the elders (7:5). Jesus warned them not to be taken in by the seductive ploy of the enemy (8:15).

Matters soon came to a head. When Jesus had cleared the temple precinct, the chief priests and teachers of the law began looking for a way to dispose of Him (11:18). They challenged His authority without success (11:28). Later they sent certain of the Pharisees and Herodians to trap Jesus concerning the paying of taxes (12:14). Still later, certain Sadducees hoped to trip Him up with a question concerning the resurrection (12:20-23). Finally, they conspired with Judas to deliver Him secretly to the authorities (14:43).

The cross on which Jesus died was situated between those of two others, perhaps also convicted of high treason.

> The term used by Mark to describe them can legitimately be translated "robbers" (see Ch. 14:48), but it is more probable that it designates men guilty of insurrection (as in Jn. 18:40). In Josephus it is constantly used for the Zealots, who committed themselves to armed conflict against Roman rule on the principle that God alone was sovereign in Israel.[99]

If so, this strikes an ironic note. Jesus' *treason* was to repudiate the institutional expression of rebellion against the Almighty. As with His disciples at a later date, in turning the world upside down, He was turning it rightside up (cf. Acts 17:6).

Jesus affirms life as redeemable. From the outset, Mark describes Jesus' mission as "good news" (1:1). In the Greek usage, good news might consist of the announcement of victory over the enemy, the birth of a child, a wedding, or oracle. Given the Hebrew precedent and present context, it seems to herald the reclamation of the world from sin.

Jesus meant to establish a beachhead from which the battle could be waged. To this end, He called disciples (1:16-20; 2:13-14). As concerns the cost, He taught that if "anyone would come after me, he must deny himself and take up his cross and follow me" (8:34).

Jesus pressed the issue relentlessly. "Be quiet!" He commanded the insolent spirit. "Come out of him!" (1:25). "Which is easier: to say to the paralytic, 'Your sins are forgiven,' or to say, 'Get up, take your mat and walk'?" Jesus asked of His carping critics. "But that you may know that the Son of Man has authority on earth to forgive sins... ." (2:9-10).

Here and there Jesus finds faith waiting. Jairus, a ruler in the synagogue, plead for Jesus to heal his daughter (5:22). As Jesus went was on His errand of mercy, a certain woman touched His garment in anticipation of being made well (5:28). A Syrophoenician woman asked to receive the crumbs that fall from the children's table (7:28). Some brought a blind man for Jesus to heal (8:22). Each time Jesus freed territory from sin's domain.

Upon the cross, Jesus cried out: "My God, my God, why have you forsaken me?" (15:34). Had God really forsaken Him? Clearly not! "It has been well said that the opening words of the cry, *My God*, are in fact in themselves an affirmation of faith. Since this same Psalm 22 from which they are quoted ends in a cry of triumph, it is reasonable to suppose that Jesus chose it with this in view also."[100]

If any doubt were to remain as to life being redeemable, the resurrection settled the matter for certain. It provided an earnest for universal deliverance.

Jesus affirms life amidst ambiguity. "The people were all so amazed that they asked each other, 'What is this? A new teaching--and with authority! He even gives orders to evil spirits and they obey him'" (1:27). What was the source of His seeming power: God, evil spirits, or slight of hand?

"Be careful," Jesus warned His disciples. "Watch out for the yeast of the Pharisees and that of Herod" (8:14). They discussed this with one another, and agreed that He referred to them not having any bread. "Why are you talking about having no bread?" Jesus wanted to know. "Do you still not see or understand?"

"Let us put up three shelters--one for you, one for Moses and one for Elijah," Peter suggested (9:5). Mark adds by way of explanation: "He did not know what to say, they were so frightened."

While the instances could be multiplied, the fact remains. Ambiguity permeates life. We should not expect it to be otherwise. Jesus takes on life in all its uncertainty.

Supporting Cast

Mark provides us with a varied supporting cast. John the Baptist is first to catch our attention. His attire consists of a roughly woven camel's hair garment, drawn in at the waste with a wide strip of leather. He subsists on a diet of locusts and honey. Both clothing and food identify him with the wilderness, as does his baptism. "The 'wilderness' motif expresses the eschatological hope of the Exodus typology found in Hos. 2:14, 12:9 and especially in Isaiah (e.g., 40:3-4; 41:18-19; 43:19-20; 48:20-21; 51:9-11). The "wilderness" represented the place where God would once again act to deliver the people."[101] John announced that the promised Savior would soon appear.

"The whole Judean countryside and all the people of Jerusalem went out to him" (1:5). Taken as hyperbolic, it corresponds with Josephus' description of the extensive impact of John's ministry (*Antiquities, 18.117*).

John fades into the background, beginning with his baptism of Jesus. This was as John had predicted (cf. John 3:30).

"John's baptism--was it from heaven, or from men?" Jesus inquired by way of response. "Tell me!" (11:30). After deliberating among themselves, Jesus' protagonists replied: "We don't know." "They feared the people, for everyone held that John really was a prophet."

The audience would greet the next figure with disdain. Satan assumes his role as adversary of God and His Christ. Having failed in his efforts to deter Jesus from His mission, Satan seems content to direct the adversarial role of his subordinates. The demons show up periodically to protest Jesus' incursion into their evil domain.

They were no match for the Master. Each time, He put them to flight.

The disciples are as a rule treated as a group. "In Mark's context, the sayings point to the fact that the crucial divide is not between those who acknowledge Jesus as the Messiah and those who do not, but between those disciples who are prepared to follow him on the way to suffering and those who are not."[102]

Even so, Jesus' disciples failed their crucial test. They slept while Jesus prayed; they fled when the security guards seized Him. They (John excluded) cowered from the authorities while Jesus' breathing became increasingly labored.

Following the resurrection, they were told to proceed into Galilee where Jesus will await them (16:7).

Perhaps in picturing the disciples as returning to Galilee--the place where they were originally called--Mark thinks of them as beginning again: they have failed Jesus, failed to take up their crosses and follow him to crucifixion, but now they are being summoned once again to follow him, and to earn once again what discipleship means. Mark may perhaps interpret the message as one of forgiveness and renewal.[103]

There were also those who shared their importunity in common. They paraded across the stage: first a man with leprosy, then a paralytic, later the first of several demoniacs, still later a dead girl, a long suffering woman, the Syrophoenician, a hungry multitude, a blind man, with anonymous multitudes.

Jesus touched the bodies of the infirm, and they were healed. He touched their spirits, and they were renewed.

The opposition came largely from the privileged. They felt threatened by Jesus egalitarian appeal. They held desperately onto what they had accumulated.

"You cannot serve both God and Money," Jesus remonstrated with them (Matt. 6:24). No one can serve two masters: for either he will hate the one and love the other, or he will be devoted to one and despise the other.

Some defy any special category. The rich young ruler illustrates how difficult it is for the affluent to answer Jesus' call to discipleship. When the centurion heard Jesus' cry from the cross and saw how He died, he declared: "Surely this man was the Son of God!" (15:39). Joseph of Arimathea, a prominent member of the Sanhedrin, went boldly before Pilate to ask for Jesus' body. These and others weave in and out of the narrative, contributing to our understanding and fortifying us to meet life's challenges undaunted.

Actors All

As reminded by William Shakespeare, "All the world is a stage and every person an actor." In keeping, Mark invites us to become involved in a sacred drama. Jesus is central. It is as we relate to Him that life takes on ultimate meaning.

Our personal agendas are of little consequence. They appear as if footprints lost in the sands of time.

The text makes a claim on us. We are to respond by repenting of our sins, and putting our faith in Christ. After this, we walk by faith and live by grace.

This resembles a *spiral*. "Those who walk it with Mark experience a new energy and a new vision. Gradually they see and perceive, hear and understand."[104]

As for the rest, they are caught in a vicious *circle*. They turn in on themselves. They are self-indulgent, sometimes under pretense of devotion to God. They rely on violence to subdue their enemies.

Mark calls for a decision. Spiral or circle, we have no other alternatives.

It is now or perhaps never. We return for a last time to consider the rich young ruler. Once he eagerly sought Jesus' counsel. When last reported, he was retreating into the distance.

Mark is about to put his pen down. "Trembling and bewildered, the women went out and fled from the tomb. They said nothing to anyone, because they were afraid" (16:8).

> This is thoroughly consistent with the motifs of astonishment and fear developed throughout the Gospel. In verse 8 the evangelist terminates his account of the good news concerning Jesus by sounding the note by which he has characterized all aspects of Jesus' activity, his healings, miracles, teaching, the journey to Jerusalem. Astonishment and fear qualify the events of the life of Jesus.[105]

So also should they qualify our ongoing experience. His is an awesome presence!

ENDNOTES

1. Aristotle, *Poetics*, Bk. 2, Ch. 1, 1448a, line 18.
2. Gilbert Bilezikian, *The Liberated Gospel*, p. 28.
3. Ibid., p. 28.
4. Ibid., p. 54.
5. R. Alan Cole, *Mark*, p. 61.
6. Robert Fowler, *Loaves and Fishes: The Function of the Feeding Stories in the Gospel of Mark*, p. 158.
7. Jerry Camery-Hoggatt, *Irony in Mark's Gospel*, p. 95.
8. Ernest Renan, "Panegyric on Jesus," *Jesus* (Anderson, ed.), p. 106.
9. Paul Kirsh, *We Christians and Jews*, pp. 34-35.
10. Richard Sewall, *The Vision of Tragedy*, p. 9.
11. H. Howard Marshall, *Acts*, p. 289.
12. Larry Hurtado, *Mark*, pp. 19-20.
13. Walter Kerr, *Tragedy and Comedy*, p. 109.
14. Ibid., p. 120.
15. William Lane, *The Gospel of Mark*, p. 50.
16. Cole, *op. cit.*, p. 110.
17. John Paulos, *Beyond Numeracy*, p. 33.
18. Ian Percival, "Chaos: A Science for the Real World," *Exploring Chaos* (Hall, ed.), p. 8.
19. Lane, *op. cit.*, p. 74.
20. Ibid., pp. 101-102.
21. Bilezikian, *op. cit.*, p. 24.
22. Annemarie De Waal Malefijt, *Religion and Culture*, p. 152.
23. Wilhelm Schmidt, *The Origin and Growth of Religion*, p. 270.
24. John Mbiti, *African Religion and Philosophy*, p. 59.
25. George Ladd, *A Theology of the New Testament*, p. 61.
26. Lane, *op. cit.*, p. 64.
27. John O'Grady, *Models of Jesus*, p. 119.
28. James Brooks, *Mark*, p. 48.

29. Joseph Weber, "Christ's Victory Over the Powers," *Above Every Name* (Clarke, ed.), p. 79.
30. James Peoples and Garrick Bailey, *Humanity*, p. 44.
31. Ibid., p. 46.
32. Donald Bloesch, *Freedom for Obedience*, p. 35.
33. Lamar Williamson Jr., *Mark*, p. 82.
34. Robert Guelich, *Mark 1-8:26*, p. 387.
35. Bilezikian, *op. cit.*, p. 76.
36. Gamery-Hoggatt, *op. cit.*, p. 105.
37. Brooks, *op. cit.*, p. 51.
38. Morris Inch, *Revelation Across Cultures*, p. 34.
39. Brooks, *op.cit.*, p. 98.
40. Yechiel Eckstein, *What Christians Should Know About Jews and Judaism*, p. 256.
41. Lane, *op. cit.*, p. 289.
42. Mary Mann, *The Construction of Tragedy*, p. 12.
43. Camery-Hoggatt, *op. cit.*, p. 142.
44. Mann, *op. cit.*, p. 12.
45. Lane, *op. cit.*, p. 304.
46. Arthur McGill, "Human Suffering and the Passion of Christ," *The Meaning of Human Suffering* (Dougherty, ed.), p. 159.
47. Joel Gajardo-Velasquez, "Suffering Coming From the Struggle Against Suffering," *The Meaning of Human Suffering* (Dougherty, ed.), p. 292.
48. John Wenham, *The Enigma of Evil*, pp. 50-86.
49. Ibid., p. 72.
50. Cole, *op. cit.*, p. 207.
51. Leon Morris, *Luke*, p. 199.
52. Robert Fuller, *Americans and the Unconscious*, p. 160.
53. George Kearns, et. al., *English Western Literature*, p. 713.
54. Lane, *op. cit.*, p. 335.
55. Kerr, *op. cit.*, p. 121.
56. Ibid., p. 123.
57. Norman Berlin, *The Secret Cause: A Discussion of Tragedy*, p. 173.
58. Richard Palmer, *Tragedy and Tragic Theory*, p. 142.
59. Brooks, *op. cit.*, p. 149.
60. Williamson, *op. cit.*, p. 170.
61. Bilezikian, *op. cit.*, p. 128.
62. Morris Inch, *Understanding Bible Prophecy*, p. 1.
63. Lane, *op. cit.*, p. 383.

64. Albert Schweitzer, "The Wind of Change," *Jesus* (Anderson, ed.), p. 140.
65. Cole, *op. cit.*, p. 272.
66. Daniel Day Williams, *The Demonic and the Divine*, p. 7.
67. Inch, *UBP*, p. 56.
68. Kearns, *op. cit.*, p. 713.
69. Cole, *op. cit.*, p. 163.
70. C. Barr Taylor and Bruce Arnow, *The Nature and Treatment of Anxiety Disorders*, p. 51.
71. Eugene Nida, *Religion Across Cultures*, p. 27.
72. Brooks, *op. cit.*, pp. 274-275.
73. Kerr, *op. cit.*, p. 124.
74. S. R. Rachman, *Fear and Courage*, p. 11.
75. Morris, *op. cit.*, p. 199.
76. Oscar Cullmann, "Immortality of the Soul or Resurrection of the Dead," *Immortality and Resurrection* (Stendahl, ed.), pp. 14-15.
77. Robert Kastenbaum, *The Psychology of Death*, p. 249.
78. C.G. Montefiore, "Jesus and the Rabbis," *Jesus* (Anderson, ed.), p. 156.
79. Palmer, *op. cit.*, p. 22.
80. Gunther Bornkamm, "Encounter with Jesus," *Jesus* (Anderson, ed.), p. 41.
81. Guelich, *op. cit.*, p. 134.
82. Inch, *RAC*, p. 23.
83. Brooks, *op. cit.*, pp. 234-235.
84. Buelich, *op. cit.*, p. 181.
85. Berlin, *op. cit.*, p. 176.
86. Robert Gundry, *A Survey of the New Testament*, p. 81.
87. Clyde Manshreck, *A History of Christianity in the World*, p. 25.
88. Berlin, *op. cit.*, p. 148.
89. Florence Dupont, *Daily Life in Ancient Rome*, p. 103.
90. Lane, *op. cit.*, p. 137.
91. Robin Fox, *Pagans and Christians*, p. 30.
92. Stephen Benko, *Pagan Rome and the Early Christians*, p. 22.
93. Williamson, *op. cit.*, p. 278.
94. William Brownson, *Meeting Jesus: Through the Good News in Mark*, p. 93.
95. Dupont, *op. cit.*, p. 122.
96. Kastenbaum, *op. cit.*, p. 258.
97. Sewall, *op. cit.*, p. 127.

98. Donald Guthrie, *New Testament Theology*, p. 221.
99. Lane, *op. cit.*, p. 568.
100. Cole, *op. cit.*, p. 321.
101. Guelich, *op. cit.*, p. 18.
102. Morna Hooker, *The Gospel According to Saint Mark*, p. 208.
103. Ibid., p. 580.
104. Robert Hamerton-Kelley, *The Gospel and the Sacred*, p. 123.
105. Lane, *op. cit.*, pp. 591-592.

BIBLIOGRAPHY

Anderson, Hugh (ed.). *Jesus: Great Lives Observed*. Englewood Cliffs: Prentice-Hall, 1967.

Berlin, Norman. *The Secret Cause: A Discussion of Tragedy*. Amherst: University of Massachusetts, 1981.

Bilezikian, Gilbert. *The Liberated Gospel*. Grand Rapids: Eerdmans, 1977.

Bloesch, Donald. *Freedom for Obedience*. San Francisco: Harper and Row, 1987.

Bornkamm, Gunther. "Encounter with Jesus," *Jesus* (Anderson, ed.), pp. 40-44.

Brownson, William. *Meeting Jesus: Through the Good News in Mark*. Grand Rapids: Baker, 1993.

Brooks, James. *Mark*, Nashville: Broadman, 1991.

Camery-Hoggatt, Jerry. *Irony in Mark's Gospel*. Cambridge: Cambridge University, 1992.

Clarke, Thomas (ed.). *Above Every Name*. Ramsey: Paulist, 1980.

Cole, R. Alan. *Mark*. Grand Rapids: Eerdmans, 1991.

Cullman, Oscar. "Immortality of the Soul and Resurrection of the Dead," *Immortality and Resurrection* (Stendahl, ed.), pp. 9-53.

Dougherty, Flavian (ed.). *The Meaning of Human Suffering*. New York: Human Sciences, 1982.

Dupont, Florence. *Daily Life in Ancient Rome*. Cambridge: Blackwell, 1993.

Eckstein, Yechiel. *What Christians Should Know About Jews and Judaism*. Waco: Word, 1984.

Fowler, Robert. Loaves and Fishes: The Function of the Feeding Stories in the Gospel of Mark. Chicago: Scholars, 1981.

Fox, Robin. *Pagans and Christians*. New York: Knopf, 1987.

Fuller, Robert. *Americans and the Unconscious*. New York: Oxford University, 1986.

Gadarjo-Velasquez, Joel. "Suffering Coming from the Struggle Against Suffering," *The Meaning of Human Suffering* (Dougherty, ed.), pp. 266-300.

Guelich, Robert. *Mark 1-9:26*, Dallas: Word, 1989.

Gundry, Robert. *A Survey of the New Testament*. Grand Rapids: Zondervan, 1970.

Guthrie, Donald. *New Testament Theology*. Downers Grove: Inter-Varsity, 1981.

Hall, Nina (ed.). *Exploring Chaos*. New York: Norton, 1991.

Hamerton-Kelley, Robert. *The Gospel and the Sacred*. Minneapolis: Fortress, 1994.

Hooker, Morna. *The Gospel According to Saint Mark*. Peabody: Hendrickson, 1991.

Hurtado, Walter. *Mark*. Peabody: Hendrickson, 1989.

Inch, Morris. *Revelation Across Cultures*. Russellville: Posey, 1995.

___. *Understanding Bible Prophecy*. New York: Harper and Row, 1977.

Kastenbaum, Robert. *The Psychology of Death*. New York: Springer, 1992.

Kerns, George, et. al., *English Western Literature*. New York: Scribner, 1987.

Kerr, Walter. *Tragedy and Comedy*. New York: DuCapo, 1985.

Kirsh, Paul. *We Christians and Jews*. Philadelphia: Fortress, 1975.

Ladd, George. *A Theology of the New Testament*. Grand Rapids: Eerdmans, 1974.

Lane, William. *The Gospel of Mark*. Grand Rapids: Eerdmans, 1974.

Malefijt, Annemarie De Waal. *Religion and Culture*. New York: Macmillan, 1968.

Mann, Mary. *The Construction of Tragedy*. Burbank: National Literary Guild, 1984.

Marshall, H. Howard. *Acts*. Grand Rapids: Eerdmans, 1991.

Maschreck, Clyde. *A History of Christianity in the World*. Englewood Cliffs: Prentice-Hall, 1985.

Mbiti, John. *African Religions and Philosophy*. Garden City: Doubleday, 1970.

McGill, Arthur. "Human Suffering and the Passion of Christ," *The Meaning of Human Suffering* (Dougherty, ed.), pp. 159-163.

Montefiori, C.G. "Jesus and the Rabbis," *Jesus* (Anderson, ed.), pp. 155-157.

Morris, Leon. *Luke*. Grand Rapids: Eerdmans, 1990.

Nida, Eugene. *Religion Across Cultures*. New York: Harper and Row, 1968.
O'Grady, Joseph. "Christ's Victory Over the Powers," *Above Every Name* (Clarke, ed.), pp. 66-82.
Palmer, Richard. *Tragedy and Tragic Theory*. Westport: Greenwood, 1992.
Paulos, John. *Beyond Numeracy*. New York: Knopf, 1991.
Peoples, James and Garrick Baily. *Humanity*. St. Paul: West, 1991.
Percival, Ian. "Chaos: A Science for the Real World," *Exploring Chaos* (Hall, ed.), pp. 11-21.
Rachman, S.R. *Fear and Courage*. San Francisco: Freeman, 1978.
Renan, Ernest. "Panegyric on Jesus," *Jesus* (Anderson, ed.), pp. 105-107.
Schmidt, Wilhelm. *The Origin and Growth of Religion*. London: Methuen, 1935.
Sewall, Richard. *The Vision of Tragedy*. New Haven: Yale University, 1980.
Stendahl, Krister (ed.). *Immortality and Resurrection*. New York: Macmillan, 1965.
Sweitzer, Albert. "The Wind of Change," *Jesus* (Anderson, ed.), pp. 140-144.
Taylor, C. Barr and Bruce Arnow. *The Nature and Treatment of Anxiety Disorders*. New York: Free, 1988.
Weber, Joseph. "Christ's Victory Over the Powers," *Above Every Name* (Clarke, ed.), pp. 66-82.
Wenham, John. *The Enigma of Evil*. Grand Rapids: Eerdmans, 1985.
Williams, Daniel Day. *The Demonic and the Divine*. Minneapolis: Fortress, 1990.
Williamson Jr., Lamar. *Mark*. Louisville: John Knox, 1983.

INDEX

Abba (Father), 77-78
    see Son of God
affirmation of life, 161-163
amazement, 74, 98, 134, 145
ambiguity, 146, 163
appearances, 106-109
audience, 74, 106, 153-160
catharsis, 137
    see audience
Celebrating Jesus as Lord, 71
chaos, 83-85, 158
complication, 71, 73, 78, 97, 103, 105
courage, 121-127
crisis, 71, 105, 109-111, 119
denouement, 71, 105, 129, 133
fear, 134, 137-143, 157
    concerning nature, 137-138
    concerning self, 140-141
    concerning society, 138-139
    concerning the supernatural, 139-140
    coping with fear, 141-143
heroic collective, 124-127
High God, 89-92
human characteristics, 97-103
    acquired, 100-103
    natural, 97-100
kingdom of God, 89, 92-95, 118, 122, 134, 150
Messiah (Christ, anointed), 72-75, 106, 114
oracles, 129-135

pity, 137, 145-151, 157
    the ethnic factor, 147
    the human factor, 145-146
    the moral factor, 146-147
    the religious factor, 147-148
prophecy, 129-133
    see oracles
reality, 105-111
Roman culture, 153-160
    concerns, 155-160
    context, 153-155
self-awareness, 140-141, 148-151
self-realization (the not as yet), 155-160
sin, 100-103
    see tragic consequences
solicited inquiry, 75
Son of God, 75-78
Son of Man, 78-80
suffering, 113-119
    in His steps, 113-116
    in community, 116-119
tragedy, 71, 89, 100, 153, 155, 161
    tragic consequence, 97-103
    tragic design, 89-95
    tragic flaw, 81-87
    tragic hero, 73-80
vigilant hope, 133-135
wilderness, 82